COOKIES & COCKTAILS

DRINK, DUNK, & DEVOUR

COOKIES
&
COCKTAILS

DRINK, DUNK, & DEVOUR

KATHERINE COBBS

TILLER PRESS

New York London Toronto Sydney New Delhi

TILLER PRESS

An Imprint of Simon & Schuster, Inc.
1230 Avenue of the Americas
New York, NY 10020

First Tiller Press hardcover edition October 2019

TILLER PRESS and colophon are trademarks of Simon & Schuster, Inc.

For information about special discounts for bulk purchases, please
contact Simon & Schuster Special Sales at 1-866-506-1949 or
business@simonandschuster.com.

The Simon & Schuster Speakers Bureau can bring authors to your
live event. For more information or to book an event, contact the
Simon & Schuster Speakers Bureau at 1-866-248-3049 or visit
our website at www.simonspeakers.com.

Conceived and produced by Blueline Creative Group LLC.
Visit: www.bluelinecreativegroup.com
Interior design by Matt Ryan
Photography by Becky Luigart-Stayner
Recipe testing by Lyda Jones Burnette
Food styling by Torie Cox
Prop styling by Mindi Shapiro

Manufactured in the United States of America

10 9 8 7 6 5 4 3 2 1

Library of Congress Control Number: 2019947282

ISBN 978-1-9821-3198-2
ISBN 978-1-9821-3199-9 (ebook)

To my parents, John Ed and Jean Withers,
consummate entertainers who kept my sister
and I well fed through the '70s and '80s
as they cooked their way through midcentury
classics by Helen Corbitt, Craig Claiborn,
Julia Child, and James Beard, and who
loved to end a great meal with a brandy
Alexander, crème de menthe over ice cream,
or a boozy coffee drink. *Cin cin* to you both.
You have always made life fun!

CONTENTS

INTRODUCTION

Milk and cookies became a "thing" for a reason. When something crumbly, warm, and sweet collides with a rich, creamy liquid, the contrasts of temperature, texture, and flavor wow the senses. Dunking a crunchy, nutty biscotti into a piping-hot cappuccino topped with a raft of milky foam satisfies in a similar way. There is delight within these culinary contradictions, but when the two come together they morph into magic. It's no wonder that people have been dunking and drinking like this for ages.

Sadly, at some point, this delightful "thing" became the stuff of kids—milk and cookies was a pairing relegated to the world of after-school snacks and treats for Santa. Meanwhile, alcohol-spiked adult cream cocktails were seen as passé—milky punches sipped by bridge-playing, cheese straw–nibbling old ladies in front parlors. Bartenders rolled eyes at Dude-wannabe requests for White Russians à la *The Big Lebowski*. It seemed that the velvety cocktail had lost its luster. Usher in a new century with the focus on waistlines, gluten sensitivities, lactose intolerances, nut allergies, and flavor-of-the-month diets, and this category of cocktails all but disappeared from radars.

Thankfully, a new era is upon us. Retro cocktails are trending– Harvey Wallbanger, anyone? And the burgeoning craft-cocktail movement is showing no signs of retreat. Like mad scientists, bartenders around the country are coming up with spirited ways to tap into milky nostalgia too. Gone are the days where cocktail menus offer up only the decadent dessert-in-a-glass standards like Mudslides, Grasshoppers, and Bushwackers. Today Momofuku Milk Bar's Cereal Milk inspires the spirited Midnight Breakfast cocktail at Birmingham's Queen's Park, proving cream cocktails can be breakfast-in-a-glass, too. At The Treasury in San Francisco, Zaytinya in Washington, DC, and Melfi's in Charleston, bartenders are using aquafaba, the whipped water from canned or cooked chickpeas, to lend the kind of froth and body to cocktails that even vegans can get behind. At Elsa in Brooklyn, rich coconut milk serves as the dairy-free base for a spiced 24 Karat Nog that has made more than a few knees buckle. Bartenders today continue to employ the age-old technique of milk

clarification, used to preserve boozy fruit punches during Colonial days, for the rich crystalline cocktail it achieves. Others are tinkering with a riff on that technique called "fat washing" to infuse booze with a wisp of rich flavor from dairy, nut or vegetable fats, and even meats (though some question the practice from a food-safety standpoint). On the commercial side, the archetypal Baileys Irish Cream has a trendy newcomer in its multiflavor lineup, Baileys Almande, that fills the ever-widening nut-milk niche. Other liqueur makers are following suit.

Whether you crave a cutting-edge milky cocktail that is a sensory surprise on every level, a milk-free spin on the classic boozy milkshake you haven't slurped in years, or a hot, soul-warming nightcap to close a perfect wintry evening, on the pages that follow, this eager sippologist brings you a sampling of dreamy drink recipes crafted to entice. Every creamy quaff is paired with a savory or sweet cookie sidekick so that you can nibble or dunk while you drink . . . the way "milk and cookies" were meant to be enjoyed. Cheers!

DAIRY IN COCKTAILS

Whoever whipped up the first milk-based cocktail with success is lost to history, but the addition of dairy likely had less to do with flavor and more to do with texture and the tempering of alcohol's burn. Just as fat carries flavor in cooking, the fat in a creamy cocktail can highlight subtle nuances in the drink, bringing out warm spicy notes or tempering overtly fruity flavors.

Beyond dairy, staples like egg yolks and egg whites are also successfully blended into liquids to provide substance, heft, and a luxurious mouthfeel. Other ingredients perform a similar function—purees of fruit, viscous sugar syrups, and potent nondairy liqueurs. In this book, the focus is on cocktails that incorporate fats from dairy (milk, cream, yogurt, and even butter), alternative dairy milks made from nuts and seeds, cream liqueurs (as opposed to crème liqueurs, *see* "Liqueur Lingo" page xii), and aquafaba (whipped chickpea water). I even slip one avocado-based cocktail in the mix because its high-fat content puts it in a league with heavy

cream and coconut milk, in my mind. Some of these ingredients weave their way into the complementary cookie sidekicks, too.

Incorporating creamy additions into your nightly tipple may seem like child's play, but there are some notable rules for emulsification success. The key to remember is that milk curdles when it comes into contact with acids like citrus. To avoid this, use fresh, full-fat cream (or alternative milks—except soy, which can also curdle) and vigorously blend or shake it to emulsify with other ingredients. Derivatives of milk, like buttermilk, yogurt, and kefir, are a bit more forgiving because they are already sour, making them more easily combined with citrus and other acidic mixtures. If a cocktail has a low acidity, then whole milk or even lower-fat dairy may be incorporated with success.

CLARIFYING METHODS
To be clear, sometimes curdled milk is desirable, at least as a step in the process of making a clarified milk

punch (*see* Here Nor There's Milk & Honey, page 8). Unlike citrus-free, creamy milk-based brandy or bourbon milk punches—such as the Whiskey-Pecan Milk Cowboy Russian (page 25) from The Kitchen at Commonplace Books—clarified milk punch uses whole milk as a means to remove impurities, color, and cloudiness from a punch, thereby extending the drink's shelf life and quality. Pouring a boozy citrus-spiked punch into a pot of hot or cold fresh milk causes the proteins in the milk to coagulate, forming a raft of curds that sinks to the bottom of the pot—a process that today is often referred to as "milk washing." Some bartenders prefer to clarify the punch base and add the booze later. The order of things depends on the flavors and traits you wish to highlight or temper in the finished punch. During the clarification process, spoilable impurities in the liquid are captured within the solids, astringent or woody flavors are neutralized, and other flavorful essences meld with more pleasing results.

Once clarified, the punch is very slowly filtered through a cheesecloth- or a coffee filter–lined sieve and refrigerated. It is not uncommon for a clarified punch to be strained multiple times before storing for months or even years. While it may seem tedious, this is a great method for making a big-batch punch cocktail in advance of an event, and it's a helpful technique for bartenders because the punch is fully mixed, stable, and ready to serve.

Of course, if curdled cottage cheese punch ever becomes a thing, you can throw caution to the wind and will know how to whip one up like a pro, no straining required.

LIQUEUR LINGO

The word "liqueur" comes from the Latin word *liquifacere* which means "to make liquid or melt." The process of making a liqueur starts by capturing and preserving the aromatic and flavorful essences of nuts, seeds, fruits, herbs, or roots in a distilled spirit base. The resulting infused spirit can become a potent, unsweetened, single-ingredient tincture or multi-ingredient bitter, but if sugar is added to the infusion, it is referred to as a liqueur or cordial. Liqueurs rose to popularity in the United States during Prohibition because they tamed the burn and bite of bootlegged spirits. They also were used in cooking. Four varying techniques are employed to produce a liqueur.

MACERATION: Through this extraction method, the chosen ingredient soaks in an unheated spirit for weeks to up to a year to permeate the liquid with flavor. The liquid is strained and blended with a neutral spirit and sometimes redistilled. The resulting "tincture" forms the base of the liqueur.

INFUSION: Temperature and time differentiate infusion from maceration. Here, raw ingredients steep in a gently heated base alcohol, which yields a flavorful result much more quickly and economically than the cold-extraction method.

PERCOLATION: This method relies on a setup that looks much like a Chemex coffeemaker or classic stovetop percolator. Ingredients are placed in a perforated chamber set over a spirit, and through pressure, a warm or cold spirit is continuously pumped over the basket. Vapor or liquid percolates back down through the raw material in the chamber, extracting flavorful essences on the journey back into the base liquid. This process may take weeks or months.

DISTILLATION: In this method, the flavoring ingredients are placed in vats of a base spirit, where they are often left to macerate for a time before being heated—often with the addition of other spirits—and distilled.

After these processes, the resulting mixtures are further "compounded" to fit a proprietary recipe. This may include filtering, blending, fining with a clarifying agent, or adding color before being sweetened and bottled. You can find liqueurs that range in potency from as low as 8% to as high as 60% alcohol by volume (ABV), with dairy-based cream liqueurs typically falling in lower ranges.

The key distinction between a liqueur and a flavored liquor is that liqueurs are spirit-based with added sweeteners unlike flavored liquors, which have no added sugars.

Crème liqueurs such as crème de menthe, crème de cacao, and crème de violette have a higher sugar content than other liqueurs, which gives them a viscous, creamy texture, but they are not to be confused with cream liqueurs. Cream liqueurs are comprised of dairy–whole milk or cream–or in some instances egg yolks or alternative milks.

COOKIE CONFIDENTIAL

I'll let you in on a little secret: Anyone can make the cookies in this book! These are not the complex confections you might find on baking competition shows, nor will you see the lengthy ingredient lists you might expect of pastry chef recipes. Each cookie on the pages that follow was crafted simply to complement the flavor profile of the cocktail with which it is paired.

WHAT MAKES A GOOD PAIRING?

Sometimes it is the yin and yang of sweet and savory. Other times it is the ingredients used to ground a duo geographically, such as pecans and bacon in a cookie paired with a Southern-style milk punch, or five-spice powder as an exotic note in a gingersnap companion for an elegant coupe infused with Southeast Asian flavor. Other times a cookie rides a wave that is similar to its cocktail companion—smoky with smoky, sweet with sweet, mint with mint, chocolate with chocolate. The takeaway here is that there really are no rules. If you want to devour a Chocolate-Almond Cookie (page 71) with the mezcal-spiked Beet Happening (page 13), go for it! Create your own magic and

trust your own palate. So raise a glass, break cookies together, and enjoy the communion of cocktail hour any way you like it.

BETTER BATCH BASICS

1. Avoid Overmixing. Mix dough just until streaks of flour disappear.

2. To Grease or Not to Grease? Grease pans only if a recipe calls for it. Better yet, forego the need altogether by using parchment or a silicone baking mat for easy cleanup every time.

3. Master Timing. Always preheat the oven. For soft, chewy cookies, remove the pan from the oven at the lower range of baking time. For crisper cookies, stick to the longer range.

4. Baking Two-Step. If baking on two baking sheets simultaneously, rotate pans halfway through baking. (For one baking sheet, center the rack in the oven for even baking.)

5. Storage. Store cookies in airtight containers or tins. Freeze cookie dough up to six months. Thaw to form and bake. Unfrosted and unfilled baked cookies can be frozen in freezer bags up to six months.

KNOW HOW TO HOLD 'EM

While outfitting a bar would be much simpler if every drink was served in the same basic glass, cocktails wouldn't be as distinctive. There is a rationale behind glass styles and how a particular shape impacts the enjoyment of a drink. The range of available glass types is broad, but below are the glasses used in this book.

STEMMED & FOOTED GLASSES

Stemmed glasses offer a place to grasp a drink, while the foot provides steady support and a bit of protection for the surface of the bar or table.

Brandy Snifter The wide balloon is meant to be cupped to warm the wine and enhance enjoyment.

Champagne Flute A conical shape reduces surface area, maintaining the wine's carbonation.

Coupe Elegant, easily spilled, this all-purpose cocktail glass is ideal for complex strained drinks served up sans ice.

Margarita Ample room for garnishes and a ring of rim salt; a version of this saucer-style glass has a unique well that helps the drinker hold the top-heavy cocktail with ease.

Martini Also called a cocktail glass, this comes in a range of sizes and is used for drinks without ice or creamy classics, like the Alexander.

Sour Also called a delmonico glass, it's narrow with slanted sides and resembles a short champagne flute, though a flared lip distinguishes it.

Wineglass Larger bowls allow the aeration and flavor development of red wines, while smaller-bowled glasses reduce oxidation, retaining the more delicate notes of white wines. Either may be used as an all-purpose cocktail glass.

Footed Pilsner The shape of this glass is designed to maintain the head of a beer, but it is also a versatile glass used for specialty drinks and cocktails.

Hurricane Taller and wider than a highball glass, this glass is named for the Hurricane cocktail and patterned after tapered glass hurricane lamps. It is often enlisted for tiki drinks like the Piña Colada.

Parfait A soda fountain staple for shakes and floats, this glass is enlisted for blended cocktails and specialty drinks.

Pousse-Café Resembling a baby parfait glass with a long stem, this small glass is for liqueurs, cordials, and layered cocktails that are meant to be slowly sipped.

TEMPERED GLASSES & MUGS

Engineered to retain heat, tempered glass mugs, much like porcelain or ceramic ones, can be preheated with boiling water before emptying to fill with a hot cocktail, while a handle allows them to be sipped comfortably.

Cappuccino Mug A five- to six-ounce mug that is typically smaller at the base and wider at the rim to accommodate a raft of steamed milk.

Irish Coffee Mug This clear mug shows off the drink's layers, while stem and base protect the bar surface. A wine goblet is also often used for serving Irish Coffee.

Mug Thick-walled to retain heat, this is a classic for hot tipples and toddies, as well as hot or cold nogs.

Teacup Daintier than a mug, this is a classic choice for a hot toddy or punch.

TUMBLERS

Collins or Fizz Tall and narrow, this straight-sided glass is tailor-made for long drinks.

Highball Tall and wider, this is the go-to for on-the-rocks drinks topped with water, soda, or a mixer.

Pearl Diver Born of the mid-twentieth century tiki drink craze, this glass was created for the Pearl Diver cocktail, but used for an array of tropical tipples or any tall drinks.

Pint Designed to hold sixteen ounces of beer, this glass has an outward taper to accommodate the foamy head of a beer, and is also used for mixed cocktails served over ice with soda, juice, or additional liquids, as well as boozy milkshakes.

Rocks This short glass is used for spirits or mixed drinks served over ice without additional soda or mixers.

Shot For tossing back a serving of liquor or for layering several types of spirits.

Stemless Wineglass This multi-purpose stemless glass is popular for its stability and versatility.

CHAPTER 1

LiGHT &

PROHIBITION

After years of bartending in New York, Jim McCourt and two fellow Belfast boys, Ray Burns and James Walsh, made the move to Charleston to open Prohibition in 2013. It's an Irish pub minus the stereotypical kitsch, known instead for its elevated food and creative cocktails with a Southern bent, served in an atmosphere that is unpretentious and inviting. Inside, rough-hewn planks of wood, black steel, and pressed-tin ceiling tiles create a multi-era mash-up of styles that works. Outside, an expansive tented patio with whiskey barrel accents and a full bar keeps the fun al fresco year round.

With close to ninety bottles, Prohibition offers the most expansive assortment of Irish whiskeys below the Mason-Dixon Line, and that's not even counting the bourbon and scotch. The fifty or so cocktails on offer change perhaps once a year, but there is always a seasonal mix thrown into the rotation. Regulars return for the perfectly executed mainstays: The Pistachio Fizz, a Bacon Maple Old Fashioned made with bacon-infused bourbon, and the 547 Manhattan with its touch of Grand Marnier so beloved by Charleston liquivores.

Lately Jim has been making his own richly-spiced horchata that he plans to spike with rum in a new cocktail offering for the upcoming menu. Of course, it's no surprise that Jim makes a mean Irish coffee that he will dose with your pick of whiskey and top with a heavy blanket of cream. He takes the classic one step further with a sprinkling of grán rósta (page 117), a housemade buttery popcorn powder that adds a welcome crunch and saltiness to the drink's boozy richness.

547 King Street
Charleston, SC 29403
843.793.2964
prohibitioncharleston.com

Pistachio Fizz

It's no wonder that this is one of the most-ordered drinks at Prohibition on Charleston's bustling King Street. It's a frothy and fizzy merging of three types of sour cocktails. It boasts the citrusy spike of the Collins, the syrupy viscosity found in the Daisy or Flip, and the egg white–and-soda etherealness of a classic creamy Fizz. Jim McCourt admits that this one is a bicep burner. A lot of shaking has to happen for Pistachio Fizz perfection. (Note: The tiny dose of xanthan gum added to the pistachio syrup keeps the nut puree suspended in the liquid, which is critical to the texture of the drink.)

1½ ounces
   Beefeater 24 gin
¾ ounce Faretti
   Biscotti liqueur
1 ounce Pistachio
   Syrup (*recipe
   follows*)
½ ounce freshly
   squeezed lime
   juice
1 ounce heavy
   cream
1 egg white
Club soda
Finely chopped
   pistachios

Add all the ingredients, except the club soda and pistachios, to a shaker tin without ice. Dry shake for 30 seconds. Add ice to the shaker and shake vigorously for 4 minutes. Strain the contents of the shaker into a chilled Collins glass filled with 1 ounce club soda. Place the drink in the freezer to chill for 2 minutes. Remove and top off with more soda just until the raft of foam rises about 1 inch above the rim of the glass. Sprinkle with the chopped pistachios.

Pistachio Puree: Drop shelled, raw pistachios in boiling water for 30 seconds. Drain and shock them in an ice bath. Remove the reddish skins by squeezing the nuts lightly between your thumb and forefinger. Puree the skinned pistachios in a high-speed blender. Alternatively, you can substitute pistachio butter (available on Amazon).

Pistachio Syrup: Bring 2 cups granulated sugar and 2 cups water to a boil in a small saucepan over medium-high heat, stirring to dissolve the sugar. Combine the sugar syrup with 3 tablespoons pistachio puree (*recipe above*) and ⅛ teaspoon xanthan gum in a high-speed blender; process for 1 minute. Transfer to a clean glass bottle. Keep refrigerated for up to 3 days. **Makes 2½ cups.**

Three Ps Sandwich Cookies

Pimento cheese, pepper jelly, and pecans collide in this savory sandwich cookie with a decidedly Southern spin. This is an adaptation of an old *Southern Living* recipe I've kept in heavy rotation, only I swap the original strawberry jam filling with zesty pepper jelly and add a pickled jalapeño on top, which slowly caramelizes to candy as the cookies bake.

1 cup pimento cheese
¼ cup (½ stick) butter, softened
1 cup all-purpose flour
½ cup finely chopped pecans

2½ tablespoons pepper jelly
Pickled jalapeño slices, drained
 and patted dry

1. Combine the pimento cheese and butter in a mixing bowl and beat with an electric mixer on medium speed until smooth. Add the flour and pecans and beat to incorporate. Turn the dough out onto a sheet of plastic wrap and flatten into a disc; wrap and chill the dough for 2 hours.

2. Center racks in the oven and preheat to 400°F.

3. Unwrap the chilled dough on a lightly floured work surface and roll it about ⅛-inch thick. Cut out 28 (2-inch) rounds. Reroll the scraps. Place 14 rounds on a parchment-lined baking sheet. Spoon ½ teaspoon of the jelly on the center of each round. Top each with one of the remaining rounds, pressing the edges to seal. Place a pickled jalapeño slice in the center on top of each cookie.

4. Bake for 13 to 15 minutes until set and golden brown. Cool on baking sheets for 5 minutes. Transfer the cookies to a rack to cool completely.

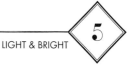

HERE NOR THERE

Austin is known for live music, bridge bats, SXSW, state politics, and the Texas Longhorns, of course. It also boasts a vibrant bar scene, catering to its diverse population of students, professionals, and tourists. Among the honky-tonks and beer joints, a handful of private speakeasies are thriving, offering the allure that comes with exclusivity.

For Dublin-born bartender Terance Robson, partner of Here Nor There, membership is about getting to know your clientele. Top-notch service predominates. Bartenders memorize patron names, faces, favorite drinks, birthdays . . . all the personal details that make membership meaningful. Keeping a finger on the pulse of member preferences, as well as aversions, allows bartenders to provide individualized service tailored to tastes. And Here Nor There is all about great taste. Terance and his talented team have built a themed bar program that changes just shy of annually and showcases an array of rare spirits. Currently drinks are inspired by global flavors, with the goal of expanding knowledge and palates.

The bar feels far from its Texas locale, which was an intentional part of its design. Just as the bar's masterful cocktails take taste buds on exotic adventures, the thoughtfully curated atmosphere—velvet, brick, brass, gleaming wood, a wall of 198 porcelain plates from around the world, and lots of Irish accents—seamlessly blends Old World and new in a way that feels perfectly now. That thought and care goes into the creation of every cocktail from glass to garnish. Some drinks, like this clarified Milk & Honey punch, took years to perfect and requires days to make, but the complexity of flavor and creamy richness prove that's neither here nor there. It's completely worth it.

612 Brazos Street
Austin, TX 78701
512.949.7995
hntaustin.com

Milk & Honey

This is an elevated version of a classic Colonial-era clarified milk punch. Milk was incorporated into an acidic punch where it would coagulate, trapping impurities. After a resting period, the mixture was fine-strained, leaving the luscious fat dispersed in a crystal-clear, silky punch. The process is used today for the richness it lends to a punch. Here Nor There's housemade Lemon Sherbet is created in a sous vide for three hours at low heat. An alternate method is provided below, but you must plan ahead.

- 1 (10½-ounce) fresh pineapple, peeled, cored, and cut into chunks
- 2 teaspoons simple syrup
- 3 drops saline solution (*see Note, page 11*)
- 6 whole cloves
- 10 coriander seeds
- ¼ teaspoon allspice berries
- 1 star anise
- 1 cinnamon stick
- 3½ ounces Batavia-Arrack
- 5 ounces Hennessy V.S.O.P Privilège cognac
- 5 ounces Daron Calvados brandy
- 2¼ ounces Blackwell rum
- 2 ounces Plantation Barbados rum (aged 5 years)
- 1¼ ounces Plantation O.F.T.D. rum
- 1½ ounces Clement Canne Bleue rum
- 3½ ounces steeped Harney & Sons Gunpowder Green tea (3 tea bags in 3½ ounces hot water)
- 7 ounces Lemon Sherbet (*recipe follows on page 10*)
- 14 ounces boiling water
- 15 ounces whole milk
- 1½ ounces lemon juice

1. Place the pineapple, simple syrup, saline solution, and all the spices in a large container. Muddle to break down the pineapple and release the flavors from the spices. Add the Arrack, cognac, Calvados, rums, and green tea. Stir in the sherbet and boiling water. Cover and let sit overnight.

2. Heat the milk in a saucepan on medium-high heat until it just comes to a boil. Pour into the container of punch. Set aside 6 hours at room temperature. Strain through a mesh strainer lined with a coffee filter into a clean container. Clean the original container and strainer. Line the strainer with a fresh coffee filter and strain again. Repeat the process until the liquid is crystal clear. Pour over ice to serve.

MAKES ABOUT 3½ DOZEN

Lemon-Lavender Icebox Cookies

Fragrant and delicious, these delicate treats are a nice change of pace from the usual cookies. Substitute crushed dried rose or hibiscus for the lavender in both the dough and glazes to change things up.

1 cup (2 sticks) unsalted butter, softened
1 cup granulated sugar
1 large egg
1 teaspoon lemon zest
2¼ cups all-purpose flour

1 tablespoon dried lavender, crushed, plus more for garnish (optional)
Generous pinch salt
Limoncello Glaze (*recipe follows*) or Fresh Lemon Juice Glaze (*recipe follows*)

1. Cream the butter and sugar with an electric mixer on medium speed until light and fluffy, 1 minute. Mix in the egg and zest to combine. Whisk together the flour, crushed lavender, and salt. Add to the wet ingredients ¼ cup at a time, until incorporated.

2. Form the chilled dough into 2 (7-inch) logs, wrap them in parchment or plastic wrap, and chill until firm, about 2 hours, or up to 3 months.

3. Preheat the oven to 350°F.

4. Slice the dough logs into ¼-inch slices and place on parchment-lined baking sheets, spacing about 2 inches apart. Bake for 12 minutes until just golden. Cool on the sheet pans for one minute. Transfer the cookies to a rack to cool completely. After cookies have cooled, spoon glaze on evenly. Sprinkle with additional lavender, if desired, and let dry completely.

Lemon Sherbet: First, make oleo saccharum by combining 7 ounces granulated sugar and 2 lemon peels in a glass jar; seal. Let sit at least 8 hours and shake the jar occasionally. Strain the syrup. To make the lemon sherbet, combine the strained syrup in another jar with 7 ounces freshly squeezed lemon juice and shake well to emulsify.

Limoncello Glaze: Whisk together 1 cup plus 1 tablespoon confectioners' sugar, 3 tablespoons Limoncello, and 1 tablespoon water in a small mixing bowl until smooth. Spoon evenly onto the center of the cooled cookies and sprinkle with 1/2 tablespoon crushed lavender. **Makes 1/3 cup.**

Fresh Lemon Juice Glaze: Whisk together 1 cup confectioners' sugar, 2 tablespoons fresh lemon juice, and 1 1/2 teaspoons water in a small mixing bowl until smooth. Spoon evenly onto the center of the cooled cookies and sprinkle with 1/2 tablespoon crushed lavender. **Makes 1/3 cup.**

NOTE: Make saline solution by dissolving 1 part sea salt in 4 parts boiling water. Cool.

OLD GLORY

Like following the Yellow Brick Road, a winding golden staircase leads visitors down into this magical Music City bar built into the bowels of an old boiler room that served a Nashville dry cleaning business for seventy years. Exposed brick, rough concrete foundation walls, electrical panels, and a soaring smokestack provide the industrial framework that the Soler sisters, Britt and Alexis, were inspired to build their second bar venture, Old Glory, around. Where many would have embarked on a gut job of the space, the Solers embraced it, tucking supple leather booths beneath balcony eaves, using gold accents to reflect rays of evening light streaming through the steel casement windows that rim the sixty-foot ceilings, and softening the rough-hewn structure with a vertical garden of green.

The regularly changing cocktail menu—another Soler sisters' collaboration—is as striking as the space. Try the earth-meets-smoke notes of the creamy Beet Happening or the fat-washed rye in the Tiki Breakfast (*recipes follow*), or stop in for the evolutionary Panther Panther cocktail, a drink that starts with a frozen cube of housemade cold brew, sweetened with demerara sugar, that gets topped with your spirit of choice. Sip after sip, the drink is transformed into something entirely new, just like Old Glory, as the flavorful ice slowly melts.

1200 Villa Place, Suite 103
Nashville, TN 37212
615.679.0509
oldglorynashville.com

Beet Happening

A vibrant Britt Soler creation—one that isn't always on the menu, but often requested. They use pebble or pellet ice in this drink at Old Glory, but crushed ice will do.

1½ ounces Banhez mezcal
1 ounce beet juice
½ ounce freshly squeezed lime juice

½ ounce house agave syrup (1 part agave syrup to 1 part water)
Bar spoon of Greek yogurt
Large dill sprig

Add everything except the dill sprig to a shaker tin. Add a small handful of crushed ice, top with a mixing glass, and shake until incorporated. Dirty dump (*see below*) into a footed pilsner glass. Fill with more crushed ice and garnish with the dill sprig.

WHAT'S IN A NAME?
"Dirty dump" refers to dumping the contents of the cocktail shaker, ice and all—without straining—into the cocktail glass to serve.

Tiki Breakfast

Bartender Kate Houser uses fat washing to infuse a base spirit with flavor and richness. Here, Nashville's Red Eye Rye, a coffee rye whiskey, gets the treatment. Houser warms up the oil to liquify and shakes it with the whiskey in a jar. After resting for 48 hours, it is refrigerated to solidify the oil for easy removal.

1½ ounces coconut fat-washed Red Eye Rye
½ ounce Smith & Cross Jamaican rum
¾ ounce lime juice

¼ ounce Salted Vanilla Demerara Syrup (*recipe follows*)
¼ ounce Giffard orgeat
Large mint sprig
1 cherry

Add everything except mint and cherry to a shaker tin. Shake with pebble ice and dirty dump into a footed pilsner. Top with pebble ice. Garnish with mint sprig and cherry.

Salted Vanilla Demerara Syrup:
Combine 2 cups demerara sugar, 1 cup water, 1 teaspoon Himalayan salt, and seeds and pod from one scraped vanilla bean in a small saucepan and cook until the sugar dissolves. Strain and transfer to a bottle. Store in the refrigerator for up to 1 month. **Makes 3 cups.**

Bacon-Chive Cornbread Madeleines

A rustic, savory version of the sweet French classic, this two-bite cornbread gets smokiness from bacon drippings and herbaceous flavor from fresh chives. These rustic bites are a favorite with brunch cocktails and taste tailor-made with smoky mezcal or whiskey drinks.

1 cup yellow cornmeal
¼ cup all-purpose flour
1 tablespoon granulated sugar
1½ teaspoons baking powder
½ teaspoon kosher salt

1 tablespoon sliced fresh chives
1 large egg, lightly beaten
1 cup buttermilk
4 tablespoons bacon grease, melted

1. Preheat the oven to 400°F. Place a 12-count madeleine mold in the hot oven to preheat for 5 minutes.

2. Combine the cornmeal, flour, sugar, baking powder, salt, and chives in a mixing bowl. Whisk together the egg and buttermilk in a separate bowl. Stir wet ingredients into dry ingredients.

3. Remove the hot madeleine mold from the oven and carefully brush the molds with 1 tablespoon bacon grease. Pour about 2 tablespoons bacon grease into the batter and stir to incorporate. Spoon about 1 tablespoon batter into each of the greased cavities of the mold and return the pan to the oven. Bake for 15 minutes until the madeleines are set and golden brown. Remove from the oven and immediately invert the pan over a rack and let cool completely.

4. Brush 8 molds of the pan with the remaining bacon grease and fill with the remaining batter. Fill the empty molds with water. Bake and cool as directed.

SABLE KITCHEN & BAR

Sable Bar is a world-class hotel bar in Chicago with an extensive whiskey and obscure spirits library that offers classic cocktails with a modern twist, while honoring the timeless traditions of the bar craft. A team of bartenders keeps the drink menu in constant evolution with a few permanent players in the mix. Creamy cocktails like Donny You're Out of Your Element—a White Russian spin using doughnut-infused vodka, St. George NOLA Coffee Liqueur, and half-and-half—stay in rotation too. Avena de Colada, a mocktail inspired by an Ecuadorian breakfast drink, combines Seedlip Grove non-alcoholic spirit, passion fruit, cinnamon, and oat milk. Those who prefer their drinks boozy can swap the Seedlip for Singani 63, a muscat-based spirit.

Veteran-bartender Brian Florczak worked his way up in the restaurant business from dishwasher to general manager by hard work and lots of independent study. An avid bargoer, reader, and podcast listener, he has built an extensive research collection of books over the years to inform his craft. This creative quaff came to him while brainstorming a new round of cocktails for Sable Bar's menu. He was inspired to develop a riff on the 1990s Spring Break standard—Sex on the Beach. Only he followed a more exotic path, taking a cue from the beaches of Dubai and the flavors of the Far East to reinvent the drink with warm-spiced soul. The resulting cocktail is as if a boozy Indian lassi tumbled into a bowl of summer berries and fragrant stone fruit. It hits all the right notes that the original never could: sweet, sour, bitter, fragrant . . . and very sophisticated.

505 North State Street
Chicago, IL 60654
312.755.9704
sablechicago.com

Sex on the Beach in Dubai

The cloying sweetness of the OG Sex on the Beach sipper is tempered by a trio of ingredients that add bright acidity—lactic acid from yogurt, citric acid from pineapple juice, and the addition of malic acid. Malic acid adds the sort of mellow, green-apple tartness you experience in a good dry white wine. Sable Bar uses housemade peach-cardamom yogurt from the restaurant's kitchen here, but you can stir a generous pinch of ground cardamom into 2 tablespoons of good-quality, whole-milk peach yogurt as a decent stand-in.

1½ ounces Ketel One vodka
½ ounce crème de cassis
½ ounce simple syrup
1 ounce pineapple juice
3 dashes saffron bitters

1 dash tiki bitters
3 dashes Malic Acid Solution
   (*recipe follows*)
2 tablespoons peach-
   cardamom yogurt

Combine all the ingredients in a cocktail shaker and dry shake to combine. Strain over a large cube of ice in a Collins glass. Garnish with a parasol.

Malic Acid Solution: Make a malic acid solution by mixing 1 part malic acid powder with 10 parts water until the powder is dissolved.

Tangerine Bars

Irresistible and simple to make, these tart-sweet treats are so versatile. Lemon is the classic, but key lime, lime, orange, or grapefruit zest and juice may be substituted to change up the flavor. Any way you make them, these bars are always a hit. The distinctive flavor of tangerine used here pairs well with whiskey cocktails, too.

2½ cups all-purpose flour
½ cup sifted confectioners' sugar, plus more for dusting
¾ cup (1½ sticks) cold butter, cut into pieces
½ teaspoon baking powder
4 large eggs, beaten

1½ cups granulated sugar
1 teaspoon grated tangerine rind
¼ cup freshly squeezed tangerine juice
1 tablespoon freshly squeezed lemon juice

1. Preheat the oven to 350°F. Line a 13 x 9-inch pan with parchment paper, allowing for a 2-inch overhang on all sides.

2. Combine 2 cups of the flour with the confectioners' sugar in the bowl of a food processor fitted with the metal blade. Pulse several times to combine. Add the butter pieces and pulse until the mixture is a coarse meal with pea-sized bits.

3. Press the flour mixture firmly and evenly into the prepared 13 x 9-inch pan. Bake for 15 to 20 minutes or until the crust is lightly browned.

4. Combine the baking powder with the remaining ½ cup flour in a separate bowl; set aside. Whisk together the eggs, sugar, tangerine rind and juice, and the lemon juice. Stir the dry ingredients into the egg mixture. Pour the filling over the warm, baked crust.

5. Return the pan to the oven and bake for 20 to 25 minutes or until lightly browned and set. Place the pan on a wire rack to cool for 30 minutes.

6. Grasp the parchment and remove from the pan. Place on the rack to cool completely. Dust lightly with confectioners' sugar. Slice into 24 bars.

THE TREASURY

In the heart of San Francisco's Financial District is an upscale bar with a Beaux Arts–Gatsby vibe. The brainchild of three partners– Arnold Eric Wong, Phil West, and Carlos Yturria–The Treasury serves elevated bar snacks and cutting-edge cocktails that incorporate the fragrant seasonal ingredients of northern California.

General Manager and bartender Ryan Hall explains, "Traditionally, the bar industry has taken a back seat to the culinary industry, but over the last decade there's been an emergence of fresh ingredients, foams, gommes, shrubs, tinctures, and infusions that can only come from astute culinary competency." The Treasury bar motto is: Everything has to have a purpose. "We walk the fine line of approachable and exciting, and it's a rewarding challenge."

For Ryan and his team of bartenders, inspiration comes from everywhere, and it's an ongoing collaborative conversation about the intersection of what's new and what's known. On a menu of sixteen cocktails and spirited slushies, six to eight drinks are seasonal offerings and the rest have been around since the bar opened.

When it comes to cocktails with richness or dairy, Ryan notes that the bar's punches are clarified with milk to circumvent perishability, while coconut milk is called into service at times for the flavor and mouthfeel it provides. Incorporating aquafaba in place of the usual egg white in sours allows the bar to recycle a byproduct of the kitchen's hummus bar snack. A recent creamy creation is The Graham cocktail. "It's our take on childhood s'mores." The centrifuged mix of bourbon, amaro, and oloroso sherry is infused with graham crackers and then fat washed with marshmallows. Consider it a liquid replica of a childhood favorite.

---

200 Bush Street, Suite 101
San Francisco, CA 94104
415.578.0530
thetreasurysf.com

Guilty Pleasure

Egg whites were the standard in creamy sours at The Treasury until new trends led the bar team to rely on the more stable aquafaba. The Guilty Pleasure is like a lot of cocktails they curate—it's about giving patrons what they want. And who doesn't love a whiskey sour? The complexity of this one is undeniable thanks to the addition of The Treasury's house blend of four complementary sherries. Amontillado provides light body, oloroso lends a slight acidity and long oaky finish, palo cortado gives more body, and the Pedro Ximénez adds fruity sweetness. As a conversation piece, bartenders garnish this drink with Angostura, using one of a handful of stencils: The Treasury logo, drake, hearts, Ron Swanson, or Air Jordan logo.

2 ounces Smooth Ambler Contradiction bourbon
½ ounce The Treasury Sherry Blend (*recipe follows*)
¾ ounce Rhubarb Gomme (*recipe follows*)
1 ounce aquafaba
¾ ounce lemon juice
Angostura (optional)

Combine all the ingredients in a cocktail shaker without ice. Dry shake. Add ice to the shaker and shake vigorously. Double strain the cocktail into a coupe, keeping the bottom of the strainer in contact with the surface of the cocktail to keep the aeration down for a smooth, velvety texture. Garnish with an Angostura flourish to serve.

The Treasury Sherry Blend: Combine 750 ml Lustau Amontillado, 750 ml Lustau Oloroso, 250 ml Lustau Palo Cortado, and 250 ml Pedro Ximénez together in a large nonreactive container. **Makes 2 liters.**

Rhubarb Gomme

1 pound rhubarb (3 to 5 stalks),
cleaned, green parts removed,
roughly chopped
15 ounces water
1¼ pounds cane sugar

2 ounces gum arabic
1 ounce citric acid
¼ ounce dried hibiscus flowers
¾ ounce rose water

1. Clip a candy or deep-frying thermometer to the side of a water-filled stockpot. Heat over medium-high heat until the water reaches 120°F.

2. Mince the rhubarb in a food processor fitted with the metal blade. Transfer it to a large ziptop bag with the remaining ingredients. Remove excess air and seal the bag. Clip the top of the bag to the side of the pot so that the ingredients are submerged. Maintain a temperature of 120°F for 2 hours. Alternatively, place the bag in a 120°F sous vide for 2 hours.

3. Strain the mixture through a fine-mesh strainer into a lidded container; cover and refrigerate until ready to use. **Makes about 2 cups.**

MAKES 1½ TO 2 DOZEN

Sugarplums

These fruit-and-nut bites are a delicious companion for The Treasury's Guilty Pleasure, or a snifter of their sherry blend.

½ cup dried mission figs,
stemmed and quartered
½ cup pitted prunes, halved
½ cup dried cherries
½ cup slivered almonds
3 tablespoons unsweetened cocoa

½ teaspoon ground cinnamon
¼ teaspoon ground allspice
⅛ teaspoon grated nutmeg
¼ cup of honey
¼ teaspoon vanilla extract
⅓ cup sanding sugar

1. Combine the dried fruits, almonds, cocoa, cinnamon, allspice, and nutmeg in the bowl of a food processor fitted with the metal blade and finely chop. Add the honey and vanilla extract and pulse a few more times.

2. Form quarter-sized balls and roll in the sanding sugar. The candies will keep up to a week in an airtight tin at room temperature.

THE KITCHEN AT COMMONPLACE BOOKS

Chris Castro didn't set out to be a bartender or a chef; life molded him into both. A first-generation American, Chris was born to Mexican parents in California. They were poor, but rich in love and laughter thanks to the connection that came with sharing every meal around the table. Chris's mom cooked exceptional dishes from humble ingredients. Friends from his high school would beg to come to his apartment to eat.

After a family move to the state, Chris attended the University of Oklahoma to study graphic design. He began cooking through his mother's recipes, impressing his roommates, friends, and girlfriend (now wife) Tricia, also an avid cook.

Later, Chris began snapping images of ingredients or the super simple meal he'd just thrown together for his young family and got noticed. He was tapped to create recipes for *Edible San Francisco* and named Cocktail Contributor for *Edible* OKC. Soon,

a buddy in the restaurant business reached out to see if Chris might partner on a kitchen and bar addition to a popular bookstore. Chris surprised himself by saying yes, and The Kitchen at Commonplace Books was born.

Chris approaches the food and cocktails in much the same way, taking his cue from the ingredients that arrive in the kitchen each morning. Something fresh and interesting might make its way into a sauce or vinaigrette, but also flavor a simple syrup to sweeten one of the unctuous sour cocktails he loves to offer. He also has a thing for infusions—especially a hibiscus-infused gin that he's been mixing with lemon juice and egg white and garnishes with a candied hibiscus flower. And, like Chris's journey to chef and bartender, there is nothing commonplace about that.

1325 N. Walker Avenue, No. 138
Oklahoma City, OK 73103
405.534.4540
commonplacebooksokc.com/kitchen

Whiskey-Pecan Milk Cowboy Russian

Chris Castro's spin on a White Russian swaps whiskey for the usual vodka, homemade coffee liqueur for the Kahlua, and uses the distinctively nutty "milk" from freshly ground, locally grown pecans in place of dairy. It's boldly flavored and dangerously drinkable.

1 ounce bourbon
1 ounce Coffee Liqueur
 (*recipe follows*)

2 ounces Pecan Milk
 (*recipe follows*)
Orange zest
Freshly grated nutmeg

Fill a shaker tin three quarters full of ice. Add the bourbon, coffee liqueur, and pecan milk. Shake vigorously until light and frothy, then strain into a rocks glass filled with ice. Finely grate a bit of orange zest and nutmeg on top with a microplane grater.

Pecan Milk

1 cup raw pecans, soaked
30 minutes and drained

4 cups water

1 teaspoon vanilla extract

1 tablespoon maple syrup

¼ teaspoon Himalayan pink salt

1. Combine the soaked pecans, water, vanilla extract, maple syrup, and salt in a high-speed blender. Blend on high for 2 to 3 minutes until creamy.

2. Refrigerate 1 hour until the liquid separates from the solids. Strain through a fine-mesh strainer into a clean quart-sized jar. Discard solids.

3. Refrigerate for up to 1 week. Shake well before serving. **Makes 1 quart.**

Homemade Coffee Liqueur

½ vanilla bean

2 cups whiskey

1 cup quality whole coffee
beans, cracked

4 cacao nibs

1 orange peel strip

1 cup simple syrup

1. Slice the vanilla bean lengthwise and scrape seeds into a clean jar. Add the whiskey and coffee beans. Cover, shake, and set aside in a cool, dark place for 24 hours. Shake from time to time.

2. After 24 hours, add the cacao nibs and orange peel to the jar. Cover, shake, and return to the cool, dark place for 24 hours more.

3. Strain the mixture through a coffee filter. Stir in the simple syrup. Store in the refrigerator up to 6 months. **Makes 3 cups.**

Maple-Pecan Sandwich Cookies with Bacon

A rich and buttery partner for Chris Castro's alt-milk whiskey punch that uses pecans from the state's abundant pecan groves. Bacon complements bourbon's smokiness, while maple tempers the sweet, caramel-y burn.

1 cup (2 sticks) salted butter, softened	2 cups all-purpose flour
½ cup granulated sugar	½ cup finely chopped pecans
⅛ teaspoon kosher salt	1 cup Maple Frosting with Bacon (*recipe follows*)
¾ cup cornstarch	

1. Center racks in the oven and preheat to 350°F.

2. Combine the butter, sugar, and salt in a mixing bowl and cream with an electric mixer on medium speed until light and fluffy, about 1 minute. Whisk together the cornstarch, flour, and chopped pecans. Add the dry ingredients ¼ cup at a time, scraping down the sides of the bowl if needed, until dough is smooth.

3. Halve the dough. Roll each portion between 2 sheets of parchment paper into a 10-inch circle, about ¼-inch thick. Transfer the rounds to the freezer for 20 minutes to firm up. Cut the chilled dough out with a 2-inch round cookie cutter. Bake, in batches, for 12 to 15 minutes, rotating the pans halfway through, until the cookies are golden at the edges. Transfer to a rack to cool completely.

4. Spread the flat sides of half of the cookies with a tablespoon of the frosting. Top with the flat side of another cookie.

Maple Frosting with Bacon

1 cup packed brown sugar	3 cups confectioners' sugar
½ cup evaporated milk	1 teaspoon vanilla extract
⅓ cup unsalted butter	4 slices cooked bacon, very finely chopped
¼ cup maple syrup	

Combine the brown sugar, evaporated milk, butter, and maple syrup in a saucepan over low heat, stirring constantly, for 5 minutes. Raise the heat to medium-low and boil for 5 minutes more. Remove from the heat. Stir in the confectioners' sugar and vanilla extract. Let the frosting cool in the saucepan for 10 minutes. Transfer the frosting to a mixing bowl and beat with an electric mixer until smooth and spreadable, 2 to 3 minutes. Fold in the finely chopped bacon. **Makes 2 cups.**

UB PRESERV

Westin Galleymore, spirits director for James Beard Award–winner Chris Shepherd's Underbelly Hospitality group, was raised by hospitality lifers. His father was owner, chef, and sommelier of the family restaurant, while his mom worked red-eye shifts as a flight attendant. Their uncommon work schedules allowed his mom to make breakfast and do the school drop-off before she slept, while afternoons were spent doing homework and helping his dad at the restaurant. His parents taught him to recognize aromas in wine and identify flavors in dishes, which honed the keen senses he relies on in his work today.

Deathly allergic to dairy, Westin doesn't shun it in cocktails on the menus of the six restaurant bars he oversees. Instead, he offers options for richly bodied cocktails that he can drink–like the eggy Flips he loves. He keeps one or two in regular rotation: the Banana Bread Flip at Georgia James or the herbaceous after-dinner sipper using Tubi 60 (a Lebanese citrus-and-herb liqueur) offered at One Fifth. He's also a fat-washing fan, washing overproof blanco tequila with sesame tahini in a White Negroni riff and mixing coconut fat-washed vodka with celery and tonic.

Asked what he would order if he could sip one final cocktail in his lifetime, Westin admits it would be a Ramos Gin Fizz. "It would definitely be my last because it would definitely kill me," he says, noting his allergy. "But I can't even begin to count how many I've made, and I am just really curious if it's actually as good as it seems."

1609 Westheimer Road
Houston, TX 77006
346.406.5923
ubpreserv.com

Time Warp

Westin gets inspiration from the giant melting pot of cultures and cuisines in Houston. This drink exemplifies that while offering a glimpse into Westin's creative process. Texans love whiskey, so he started there. Agua de Jamaica, a Mexican sweetened hibiscus tea, is sipped by many to quell Houston's intense summer heat. Finding a way to marry these disparate ingredients took experimentation. He considered how pear is a flavor note found in some whiskeys, and fruit and hibiscus play well together, but he also wanted the drink to have a Piña Colada texture and remain dairy-free. He needed a supporting ingredient to bridge the gap. Vanilla soy yogurt proved to be the luscious link. This recipe makes a large batch of syrup, which is delicious stirred into iced tea or seltzer water.

2 ounces bourbon
1 ounce Silk vanilla soy yogurt

¾ ounce Hibiscus Pear Syrup
(*recipe follows*)
2 thin pear slices

Dry shake the bourbon, yogurt, and syrup in a shaker tin to combine. Pour over ice in a hurricane glass or footed pilsner. Garnish with the pear slices.

Hibiscus Pear Syrup: Heat 4 cups pear juice, 4 cups water, and 8 cups granulated sugar in a large saucepan until hot, but not boiling. Stir until the sugar dissolves. Remove from the heat and add 1 cup, plus 2 tablespoons dried hibiscus flowers. Steep at least 15 minutes prior to straining. Strain and transfer to a bottle. Keep refrigerated for up to 1 week. **Makes 8 cups.**

WHAT'S IN A NAME?
The Time Warp is space-time distortion in a glass. It conjures Deep South, Colonial bourbon milk punches, while revealing something completely new and unexpected upon first sip.

Pepita Wedding Cookies

Mexican wedding cookies—also referred to as Russian tea cakes or snowballs—are traditionally made with pecans. Here, pepitas—hulled pumpkin seeds—are a nice swap to complement Westin's creative Time Warp cocktail. For a dairy-free cookie, substitute coconut oil for the butter in this recipe.

½ **cup (1 stick) butter, softened**
¼ **cup confectioners' sugar, plus more for rolling**
1 **teaspoon vanilla extract**
1 **cup plus 2 tablespoons all-purpose flour**

½ **teaspoon salt**
⅛ **teaspoon ground cinnamon**
½ **cup finely chopped roasted and salted pepitas**

1. Preheat the oven to 400°F.

2. Beat the butter with an electric mixer on medium speed for 2 minutes. Add the confectioners' sugar and beat until creamy, about 3 minutes. Add the vanilla. Stop to scrape down the bowl as necessary.

3. Combine the flour, salt, cinnamon, and chopped pepitas in a separate bowl. Gradually add the dry ingredients to the butter mixture just until incorporated.

4. Roll the dough into 1-inch balls and place on parchment-lined baking sheets. Bake for 10 to 12 minutes. Remove the cookies to a wire rack to cool slightly. Roll the warm cookies in confectioners' sugar and return to the wire rack to cool completely.

ZAYTINYA

The flavors and aromas of the Mediterranean greet you at Zaytinya, located in the vibrant and eclectic Penn Quarter neighborhood in Washington, DC. The mezze menu celebrates the ingredients and cuisines of Turkey, Lebanon, and Greece with dishes inspired by Chef José Andrés' travels throughout the region.

While an expansive wine list takes you on a tour of Mediterranean terroir, the cocktail menu is a serenade to the varied flavors that inspire the region's many cuisines. Miguel Lancha, cocktail innovator for Chef Andrés' restaurant group, explains that garbanzos or chickpeas are an integral part of the culinary heritage of the Mediterranean. Using the bean water, or aquafaba, is a way to give cocktails body, but also an opportunity to infuse them with yet another subtle flavor of the region.

"It really is not neutral as many think. The aroma of the chickpea is present and adds to the overall experience of the drink," Miguel stresses. He also notes that while the use of aquafaba is partly about rooting the cocktail to place, there is the added bonus that it is an ingredient that remains stable and won't break down like egg whites eventually do in cocktails.

Though Zaytinya's bartenders do use cream and vanilla syrup in a spin on a Ramos Gin Fizz, and turn to milk to clarify punch bases from time to time, dairy doesn't figure prominently in cocktails at the restaurant because the chef likes to keep things "sour, crispy, clean, and light," as Miguel puts it. That's just what you'll find in Zaytinya's Tsipouro Sour.

701 9th St NW
Washington, DC 20001
202.638.0800
zaytinya.com

Zaytinya's Tsipouro Sour

This is a classic sour with a Greek twist. Tsipouro, a traditional Greek brandy distilled from grapes, stands in for the usual gin or whiskey.

1½ ounces tsipouro, like Katsaros
¾ ounce simple syrup
¾ ounce freshly squeezed lime juice
2 dashes orange blossom water
1 ounce aquafaba (chickpea water)
3 dashes Angostura bitters

Combine all the ingredients, except the bitters, in a shaker tin. Dry shake vigorously for 30 seconds. Add ice to the shaker and shake for 30 seconds more. Strain into a chilled coupe glass. Garnish the foam with three dashes of Angostura bitters. Drag a toothpick through the bitters to make a design in the top of the cocktail froth, if desired.

WHAT'S IN A NAME?
Zaytinya refers to the José Andrés restaurant where this is served. It is the Turkish word for olive oil.

Manchego-Membrillo Thumbprints

Perhaps because Miguel and his boss both hail from Spain, this slightly smoky spin on a savory cheese thumbprint cookie came to my mind. I used nutty Manchego cheese in the dough and membrillo, a paste made from quince, for the filling. This Spanish spin on a cheese biscuit is delicious with a glass of wine or wine-based cocktails—even if the wine is Greek.

- ¾ **cup (1½ sticks) salted butter, softened**
- 3½ **tablespoons honey**
- 2 **cups all-purpose flour**
- 1 **cup (2½ ounces) grated Manchego cheese**
- 1 **teaspoon smoked paprika**
- ½ **teaspoon salt**
- 1 **(10-ounce) container quince paste, cubed**
- 1 **tablespoon lemon juice**

1. Preheat the oven to 350°F. Line 2 baking sheets with parchment paper and set aside.

2. Combine the butter and honey in a mixing bowl. Cream the ingredients with an electric mixer on medium speed until light and fluffy, about 3 minutes. Mix together the flour, grated cheese, smoked paprika, and salt in a separate bowl. Gradually add the dry ingredients to the wet ingredients. Stop to scrape down the sides of the bowl as necessary. Beat just until the dough comes together.

3. Shape the dough into 1-inch balls and refrigerate for 1 hour. Arrange on the prepared baking sheets, spacing about 2 inches apart. Lightly press a thumb or the back of a teaspoon into the center of each cookie to make an indentation. Bake for 10 to 12 minutes, rotating the pans halfway through baking. Transfer the cookies to a rack to cool completely.

4. While the cookies cool, process the quince paste and lemon juice in a food processor. Spoon the mixture into the center of each cooled cookie.

MELFI'S

Restaurant partners Brooks Reitz and Tim Mink create experiences. The two are involved in every detail of their restaurant ventures from concept to completion and it shows. Melfi's is all about bringing truly terrific pizza and a bit of Italian authenticity to Charleston.

Exposed brick walls, a curvaceous leather banquette, handsome bar, classic lighting, and crisp white tablecloths make the restaurant feel as though it's been in the neighborhood for generations. The duo managed to infuse the space with the same sort of timeless ambience they so masterfully cultivate at their Leon's Oyster Shop and Little Jack's Tavern restaurants too.

Melfi's serves small plates, salads, pasta, and thin-crust "à la Romana"–style pizzas, many of which have witty names that could be cocktails:

Mr. Wally, a nod to the Wallbanger for its vodka sauce, perhaps? Or the Stretch Armstrong, a reference to the stretchy stracciatella cheese used on a classic margherita pie.

As the visionary behind the Jack Rudy Cocktail Company—named for his grandfather—Reitz is well schooled in the shake, rattle, and pour behind the bar, and the cocktail menu reflects his side business, creativity, and the restaurant's Italian theme. Melfi's offers your choice of Italian beers, plenty of amaro cocktails, several boozy riffs on Italian Shakeratos, and half a dozen spins on the Negroni, including this sour twist that Melfi's bartenders shake with aquafaba.

721 King Street
Charleston, SC 29403
843.513.0307
eatatmelfis.com

Dr. Melfi's Medicine

This bitter cocktail is hardly a tough pill to swallow; it's a classic Negroni given the Sour treatment. Brooks Reitz prefers the clean flavor of aquafaba to egg white in sours.

½ ounce **Campari**
½ ounce **Beefeater**
½ ounce **Martini & Rossi sweet vermouth**

¾ ounce **lemon juice**
½ ounce **simple syrup**
½ ounce **aquafaba**
orange peel for garnish

Combine all the ingredients in an ice-filled shaker tin. Shake vigorously and double strain into an ice-filled Collins glass.

WHAT'S IN A NAME?
Melfi's is named for the Italian American family who came to Charleston in the 1800s and owned the pharmacy that used to occupy the space. The family's coat of arms is framed on the wall at the restaurant.

Prosciutto-Wrapped Dates

Yes, to call these "cookies" might be a stretch, but since dates are tiny sugar bombs in their natural state, it doesn't seem so far-fetched. This nibble stuffs and wraps the sweet, sticky fruit for an umami-herbaceous appetizer that's divine with bitter amaro cocktails like Dr. Melfi's Medicine.

12 pitted Medjool dates
1½ ounces (3 tablespoons) mascarpone cheese, at room temperature
1½ ounces (3 tablespoons) Gorgonzola crumbles, at room temperature

Pinch kosher salt
Pinch freshly ground black pepper
6 very thin slices prosciutto, halved lengthwise
2 teaspoons balsamic glaze
Fresh thyme leaves

1. Preheat the oven to 350°F. Line a baking sheet with parchment paper.

2. Slice the dates lengthwise without cutting all the way through the fruit and set aside.

3. Combine the mascarpone, Gorgonzola, salt, and pepper in a small bowl and mash with a fork to blend. Spoon about 1½ teaspoons of the cheese mixture into the center of each date and pinch closed. Wrap tightly with a belt of prosciutto to secure. Place the dates on the prepared baking sheet and bake for 15 to 20 minutes, turning halfway through.

4. Remove the dates and drizzle each with a few drops of balsamic glaze and a few thyme leaves. Serve warm.

CHAPTER 2

RiCH &

CREAMY

PALEY'S PLACE

Paley's Place is a restaurant at the forefront of Pacific Northwest cuisine—a cuisine that reflects the mosaic of cultures that make up the region, using seasonal ingredients that are fished, foraged, and farmed nearby.

Bar manager Charlie Gleason approaches cocktails in a similar fashion, always looking to strike a balance between familiar ingredients and flavors, and the excitement of the unknown. Cocktails here are often new takes on enduring classics, but rarely include more than a handful of ingredients. "With only one bartender during service who makes every drink for the restaurant, I keep labor-intensive ingredients minimal to ensure cocktails are quick and easy to construct," she says. The offerings change as seasonal ingredients pop up or she or the other bartender come up with something new and fun.

Her pet peeve: customers who order martinis with no vermouth. "A vodka or gin martini without vermouth is simply a chilled glass of vodka or gin. If that's what you want to drink, I'll make it straightaway and serve it with a smile, but it's not a martini. Plus, vermouth is delicious! I'm on a mission to foster appreciation for vermouth."

When it comes to full-bodied cocktails, Charlie admits she is an avoider of industrialized thickeners and unknown ingredients, so avoids commercial alt-dairy products and cream liqueurs. As far as the fat-washing trend, she notes that washing spirits with animal fats can be risky business, but she has washed tequila with coconut oil to great success. Charlie finds that fruit purees and syrups are a wonderful way to give body to cocktails, specifically the pectin in cranberries and pears as well as citrus oils. In her Sofia Cocktail she enlists all three: fruit, syrup, and citrus, plus a bar spoon of yogurt for milky measure.

1204 Northwest 21st Avenue
Portland, OR 97209
503.243.2403
paleysplace.net

Sofia Cocktail

Charlie suggests White Mountain Bulgarian yogurt here, but you may substitute a plain yogurt of your choice. Gin's juniper base pairs beautifully with sweet, herbaceous Combier Kümmel's notes of caraway, fennel, and cumin in this cocktail with lots of vegetal complexity.

2-inch strip lime peel
2 to 3 mint leaves
2 to 3 kaffir lime leaves, plus 1 for garnish
¼ ounce agave syrup (2:1 agave to water)
2 ounces Tanqueray N° TEN gin

¼ ounce Combier Kümmel liqueur
10 drops or a few dashes cucumber bitters
Heaping bar spoon Bulgarian yogurt

Muddle the lime peel, mint, and lime leaves with agave in a cocktail shaker. Add the gin, Kümmel, bitters, yogurt, and a handful of ice, and shake vigorously for 15 to 20 seconds. Double strain into a coupe glass and garnish with an additional lime leaf.

WHAT'S IN A NAME?
The Sofia Cocktail is a direct reference to the capital of Bulgaria. Charlie loved knowing that there was this unbelievably delicious strain of bacteria specific to Bulgaria that makes the yogurt there taste like no other.

Five-Spice Gingersnaps

Gingersnaps are a teatime classic that should become one for cocktail hour, too. Clove, fennel, star anise, cinnamon, and peppercorn are the five spices that weave their way into this not-too-sweet cookie—a medley of flavors that work beautifully with the exotic notes in the cocktail. Swap the five-spice powder for pumpkin pie spice, ground cardamom, or cinnamon to change up the flavor profile to suit your taste or tipple.

2 cups all-purpose flour
1 tablespoon ground ginger
2 teaspoons baking soda
½ teaspoon salt
1½ teaspoons Chinese five-spice powder

½ cup (1 stick) butter, softened
¾ cup granulated sugar
¼ cup sorghum
1 large egg

1. Combine the flour, ginger, baking soda, salt, and five-spice powder in a medium bowl. Mix the butter, ½ cup of the sugar, and the sorghum with an electric mixer on medium speed until smooth. Add the egg and beat to incorporate. Add the dry ingredients in batches, beating well after each addition. Freeze the dough for 1 hour or until firm.

2. Preheat the oven to 350°F.

3. Roll the chilled dough into 1-inch balls. Dip one side of each dough ball in the remaining ¼ cup granulated sugar and place 2 inches apart on parchment-lined baking sheets, sugar side up. Bake for 10 to 12 minutes, until brown and cracked on the surface. Cool cookies on the baking sheet for 2 minutes before transferring to a wire rack to cool completely.

SATURN ROOM

A tiki bar in Tulsa may seem as out of place as grass skirts at a rodeo, but the fact that the Saturn Room is regularly filled to capacity proves it's the perfect little throwback bar on the Oklahoma prairie.

Situated in the vibrant Brady Arts District, a wall of windows opens behind the bar to the patio with its expansive view of the Tulsa skyline beyond. Inside, booths are trimmed in bamboo, woven grasscloth lines the walls, and a thatched roof covers a bank of tables, giving the space an irresistible Don the Beachcomber vibe at every turn.

Bartenders serve upward of fourteen hundred glasses of the bar's most popular drink, the Macadamia Nut Chi Chi, each month. General Manager Gavin Hatcher says the Chi Chi is so popular because of the quality of the ingredients that they use. Behind the bar, fresh coconuts are carefully cracked open, and the milky coconut water and rich coconut meat scraped from the shell get pureed in the pitcher of a high-speed blender. A bit of sugar is added to the mix and it's blended into the frothy frappé that serves as the creamy base of the cocktail, which sets this decadent drink apart from the usual bottled coco-blend tiki tipples. Well, that and the fact that this top-quality creamy tiki drink comes to you from Tulsa.

209 N Boulder Avenue
Tulsa, OK 74103
918.794.9422
saturnroom.com

Macadamia Nut Chi Chi

If the coconut shell doesn't shatter when cracked open to make the coconut cream, Saturn Room bartenders will serve the drink in a coconut shell, otherwise a stemless wineglass and orchid garnish will have to do. It may seem like a liquor cabinet outlier, but the macadamia nut liqueur is worth the purchase. It has the distinctive nutty flavor of toasted macadamia nuts with hints of vanilla and caramel. Use it as you would Frangelico or Amaretto in coffee, or drizzle it over ice cream, and you'll impress with the twist of a bottle cap.

1 ounce fresh (*recipe follows*) or canned coconut cream
1¼ ounces Trader Vic's Macadamia Nut liqueur

2 ounces vodka
4 ounces pineapple juice
1 cup crushed ice
1 orchid blossom, for garnish

Add all the ingredients into a blender with the crushed ice and blend on high. Pour into a coconut shell or stemless wineglass and garnish with a pink orchid.

Homemade Coconut Cream: Crack open a medium fresh coconut and pour the liquid into the base of a high-speed blender. You will have anywhere from ½ to 1 cup liquid. Scrape out the coconut flesh and add it to the blender (you should have about 10 ounces coconut meat) with a few tablespoons granulated sugar. Whirl the contents on high until thoroughly blended.

Coconut-Banana Macaroons

These macaroons get a double dose of island flavor with coconut and banana in the mix. Turn these into macaroon sandwiches by slathering Nutella on the flat side of one and pressing with the flat side of another.

¼ cup mashed ripe banana
  (about 1 medium banana)
2 large egg whites
⅓ cup granulated sugar

¼ teaspoon Himalayan pink salt
½ teaspoon vanilla extract
1 (14-ounce) package
  sweetened shredded coconut

1. Preheat the oven to 325°F.

2. Whisk the banana, egg whites, sugar, salt, and vanilla extract to combine. Fold in the coconut with a spatula until incorporated.

3. Drop by rounded tablespoonfuls, about 1 inch apart, on two parchment-lined baking sheets. Bake for 20 minutes or until light golden brown. Transfer to a rack to cool completely. Store for up to 1 week in an airtight container.

FLORA-BAMA

The iconic Flora-Bama, often called "America's Last Great Roadhouse," opened in 1964 and has remained a regular stop for beachgoers, bands, and locals ever since. Though its official address is in the state of Florida, the bar straddles the Alabama-Florida border at Orange Beach and Perdido Key. Whether it's Bingo Night or Taco Tuesday, the bar draws patrons every day of the week. You can even attend church there on Sunday mornings, head home for a siesta, and return after sunset for S.I.N. (Service Industry Night), to fill up on cocktails and food at employee prices.

Whether you're in town for the annual Mullet Toss or a contestant in Destin's Fishing Rodeo, when it's ninety-five degrees outside with relative humidity to match, it's as dangerously easy to suck down the bar's Bushwacker as it is a drive-thru milkshake . . . so slurpers beware! The Flora-Bama's adult shake includes two kinds of rum, a double dose of liqueur, milk, and ample sugar to buffer the booze. It's a midsummer day's nap in a cup (and potentially *tomorrow's* hangover too), guaranteed to leave you . . . well, bushwacked should you proceed without caution.

Long ago, the bar perfected the large-scale Bushwacker base that gets mixed with milk in frozen drink machines, so that the bar always keeps the good times churning. On rare occasions when the milk runs out, like busy Fourth of July holidays, employees have been known to clean out the dairy shelves of the neighboring Winn-Dixies on both sides of the border to ensure that no one who stops in at the Flora-Bama ever goes without. Now you don't have to either.

17401 Perdido Key Drive
Perdido Key, FL 32507
850.492.0611
florabama.com

Flora-Bama Bushwacker

The Flora-Bama recipe is large-batch and top secret, but these are the components, scaled for one drink, using ice cream in place of the milk that freezes as it churns in the bar's drink machines. If you prefer, lose the ice cream and mix everything with 1 cup milk, half-and-half, or heavy cream in an ice-filled shaker instead.

1 ounce white rum
1 ounce dark rum
1 ounce Kahlua

1 ounce crème de cacao
2 scoops vanilla ice cream
1 Maraschino cherry

Combine everything in a high-speed blender and blend for 30 seconds. Pour into a pint glass and serve with a straw and garnish with a cherry.

White Chocolate-Cherry-Pistachio Oatmeal Cookies

White chocolate lends creaminess to these chunky drop cookies, plus its neutral flavor lets bright cherry and distinctive pistachio shine.

½ cup dried cherries
¼ cup plus 1½ tablespoons kirsch
½ cup (1 stick) unsalted butter, softened
¼ cup granulated sugar
⅓ cup packed dark brown sugar
1 large egg

1 cup all-purpose flour
½ teaspoon baking soda
¼ teaspoon ground allspice
⅛ teaspoon kosher salt
1 cup rolled oats
½ cup white-chocolate chips
½ cup shelled pistachios, chopped

1. Center racks in the oven and preheat to 375°F.

2. Combine the cherries, ¼ cup of the kirsch, and 3 tablespoons boiling water in a bowl. Set aside for 20 minutes to allow the fruit to plump up.

3. Combine the butter and sugars in a stand mixer fitted with the paddle attachment. Starting on low speed, cream the mixture by gradually increasing the speed to high until it is fluffy, about 3 minutes. Mix in the egg and the remaining 1½ tablespoons kirsch (or substitute 1 teaspoon cherry extract). Stop to scrape down the sides of the bowl as necessary.

4. Whisk together the flour, baking soda, allspice, salt, and oats in a medium bowl. Gradually add the dry ingredients into the wet ingredients, stirring with a wooden spoon until combined. Fold in the white-chocolate chips and pistachios. Drain and fold in the cherries to evenly distribute.

5. Drop rounded tablespoonfuls of dough onto two parchment-lined baking sheets, spacing 2 inches apart. Bake for 12 minutes, until the edges are golden brown. Let cool on the pans for 1 minute. Transfer to a rack to cool completely. Store in an airtight tin at room temperature for up to 1 week.

ELSA BAR

Natalka Burian had worked in the hospitality industry for years, running a dive bar with a good friend in the East Village, when her business partner made some life changes and galloped off to Texas. Natalka decided to partner with her boyfriend (now husband), Jay Schneider, and embark on an entirely new bar concept. Together they reimagined and transformed the old dive bar into what became the original Elsa Bar on East Third Street. Weary of the hypermasculine energy and pre-Prohibition vibe permeating the bar scene at the time, the two recognized the need for a bar atmosphere that was more inclusive, fresh, and fun.

Naming their new venture felt as important as naming a baby. The two wanted a name that would reflect the feminine, enchanted mood of the space that they created together. The name Elsa seemed perfect—a soft,

lovely name to personify a similar space and set a welcoming tone. Though the OG Elsa closed a handful of years ago, a younger Elsa was born in Brooklyn in 2017 not far from sister bar Ramona. Neither Natalka nor her husband works behind the bar these days, but they remain very hands-on in the day-to-day operations of both Brooklyn locations.

One of Elsa Bar's talented bartenders, Margaret Fitzjarold, developed this eggless, alt-dairy nog recipe. Though it's completely vegan, you still get that silky, lush, creamy effect without the accompanying heaviness or sense of overindulgence that you get with from traditional egg-and-dairy nog.

136 Atlantic Avenue
Brooklyn, NY 11201
917.882.7395
elsabarnyc.com

Elsa Bar 24 Karat Nog

This is a very user-friendly recipe for entertaining at home. It's simple to throw together and you don't have to worry about the possible contamination of using raw eggs.

2 ounces navy rum
2 ounces coconut milk
½ ounce coconut cream,
  preferably Coco López

Generous pinch Spice Mix
  (*recipe follows*)
½ ounce maple syrup
Chili oil, ground cinnamon,
  or fresh nutmeg

Shake the rum, coconut milk, coconut cream, pinch of spice mix, and maple syrup in an ice-filled shaker. Single strain into a mug or glass and garnish with a few drops of chili oil, a sprinkle of ground cinnamon, or grating of fresh nutmeg.

Spice Mix: Combine 1 teaspoon ground cinnamon, 2 teaspoons freshly grated nutmeg, and 3 teaspoons ground turmeric. Store in a jar with a tightfitting lid for 3 months.

WHAT'S IN A NAME?
Feminine and strong, Elsa was a fitting name for the inviting bar that Natalka and Jay created and continue to cultivate. The 24 Karat Nog gets its name from the golden spice mix that infuses the drink.

Buttery Tuiles

You can form these warm cookies into an array of shapes—cones, *tulipes* or cups, or cigars. A silicone baking mat is key here. Serve this versatile cookie unadorned with fizzes, sours, and such. Or use Irish cream filling (page 59), or sorbet or ice cream to serve with after-dinner drinks. Select your preferred extract here to skew the flavor any which way you wish.

2 large egg whites
½ cup granulated sugar
½ teaspoon flavored extract

¾ cups all-purpose flour
⅓ cup (5 tablespoons) butter, melted

1. Whisk the egg whites, sugar, and extract of choice until well mixed but not foamy. Whisk in the flour and then the melted butter until incorporated. Refrigerate the batter for 2 hours.

2. Preheat the oven to 350°F. Line a baking sheet with a silicone baking mat or parchment.

3. Place a level tablespoon of batter to one side of the baking sheet, several inches from the edge (the batter will be thick). Spread the batter into a very thin (4- to 5-inch) round with the back of a spoon or an offset spatula. Repeat two more times. (Make no more than 3 tuiles at a time because you must form them as soon as they come out of the oven while warm.)

4. Bake the tuiles until lightly brown but still pliable, 5 to 6 minutes. Using a spatula, peel the tuiles from the parchment and drape them over a rolling pin or juice glass to create the curved tuile shape. When cool, remove the cookies and store for up to 1 week in an airtight tin.

NOTE: If the tuiles cool before you have a chance to form them, place them back in the oven for 20 seconds or so to soften, so that you can shape as desired.

Variation: To make tulips, simply transfer the warm cookies from the sheet pan and drape over an inverted Pyrex custard cup or ramekin. To make cones, form crumpled foil into a small cone form and wrap the warm cookie around the foil cone.

Irish Cream Filling

4 ounces mascarpone cheese,
  at room temperature
3 tablespoons confectioners'
  sugar

¼ cup Baileys Irish cream
½ cup whipped cream

Combine the mascarpone, sugar, and Irish cream in a bowl and beat on medium speed until light and creamy. Fold the whipped cream into the mixture to lighten. Spoon the mixture into the tuile cones, cups, or cigars.

WHAT'S IN A NAME?
The word *tuile* is French for "tile" and refers to the delicate curve of the cookies that is reminiscent of the clay roof tiles found on buildings throughout the Mediterranean.

TUJAGUE'S

Nestled in the French Quarter, Tujague's (pronounced two-jacks) is the second oldest restaurant in New Orleans and the oldest stand-up bar in America, which means there are no barstools flanking the expansive bar top. Tujague's is a landmark institution where both brunch and the Grasshopper cocktail were born and endure. It's said to be the home of several lingering spirits, too, including a previous Tujague's owner, and a cross-dressing star of silent film.

Opened by Guillaume Tujague in 1856 at 811 Decatur Street, Tujague's was the French immigrant's second successful business in New Orleans after his popular French Market food stall made him wealthy. The original Tujague's was situated a few doors down from the bustling Begue's Exchange, an eatery where market hall workers, butchers, and bakers enjoyed lavish after-shift breakfasts, no matter the time of day. Because Madame Begue's tiny dining room could only hold so many, Tujague's became the default beneficiary of the overflow. Guillaume capitalized on this by adding an any-time-of-day butcher's breakfast to his own menu.

Though the restaurant has changed hands many times over the years, its reputation has held its own. Current owner, Mark Latter, took over from his father. He kept many menu items and longstanding traditions, but created new ones too. It's a balance that has kept Tujague's relevant for generations, and it's what makes it a place where milestones are celebrated, holiday feasts enjoyed, Grasshoppers sipped, and the dearly departed stick around.

823 Decatur Street
New Orleans, LA 70116
504.525.8676
tujaguesrestaurant.com

Tujague's Original Grasshopper

This creamy yet refreshing concoction was created by the second owner of Tujague's, Philibert Guichet. It placed second in a 1919 cocktail competition in New York City and became so popular in New Orleans that it has remained a mainstay on Tujague's menu ever since. It also serves as inspiration for the ever-popular grasshopper pie. In the Midwest, you'll find Grasshoppers blended with ice cream instead of shaken with cream, but rest assured, the recipe below is straight from the source. Today, Tujague's uses Bols brand liqueurs in its Grasshoppers.

1 ounce white crème de cacao
½ ounce dark crème de cacao
½ ounce green crème de menthe
¼ ounce white crème de menthe
⅛ ounce brandy plus ½ teaspoon brandy for garnish (optional)
2½ ounces heavy cream

Combine everything in an ice-filled shaker tin. Shake vigorously. Strain into a champagne flute. Float ½ teaspoon brandy on top to garnish, if desired.

Mint Chocolate Chip Cookies

It's hard to beat a classic chocolate chip cookie. It begs to be eaten before it has even cooled (or for many, before it has even been baked), and its nooks and crannies are like a sponge for ice-cold milk. Somehow this mint chocolate version seems refreshingly acceptable, especially for dunking in a minty Grasshopper.

½ cup (1 stick) butter, softened
¾ cup granulated sugar
½ cup packed dark brown sugar
2 teaspoons vanilla extract
2 large eggs

2½ cups all-purpose flour
1 teaspoon baking soda
1 teaspoon baking powder
1 teaspoon salt
1 (10-ounce) bag Andes crème de menthe baking chips

1. Preheat the oven to 350°F.

2. Combine the butter and sugars in the bowl of a stand mixer fitted with the paddle attachment, starting on low speed. Cream the mixture by gradually increasing the speed to high until the mixture is light and fluffy, about 3 minutes. Add the vanilla extract and the eggs, one at a time until blended. Scrape down the sides of the bowl as necessary.

3. Whisk together the flour, baking soda, baking powder, and salt in a medium bowl. Gradually add the dry ingredients into the wet ingredients, stirring with a wooden spoon until combined. Fold in the baking chips to evenly distribute.

4. Drop rounded tablespoonfuls of dough onto two parchment-lined baking sheets, spacing about 2 inches apart. Flatten slightly with the bottom of a juice glass or clean palm. Bake for 8 to 10 minutes until golden brown. Let cool on the pans for 2 minutes. Transfer the cookies to a rack to cool completely. Store for up to 1 week in an airtight tin at room temperature.

LA FABRICA CENTRAL

Chef Giovanna Huyke is often referred to as the Julia Child of Puerto Rico. She was born into a family with a zest for life and passion for food and travel. Her parents worked tirelessly in order to enjoy their leisure. Sundays were all about family from sunrise to sundown, endcapped by the big Sunday dinner her mom always prepared.

Giovanna's mom was a chemist who'd dreamed of becoming a chef at a time when culinary schools in Europe didn't accept women. Her mother's love of food plus her studious mind made her a great cook even so, and she became a celebrated culinary teacher in Puerto Rico. Giovanna was a lucky beneficiary. At family Sunday dinners there was always plenty of food and an extra seat for the friends and extended family who inevitably stopped by. Giovanna's father, also a consummate host, picked out wines and selected music to ensure that every meal was a special occasion.

While in college in New Orleans, Giovanna landed a job as assistant to the famed chef Paul Prudhomme. His kitchen became her incubator for a lifelong career in restaurants. She went on to run several in Puerto Rico, New York, Washington, DC, and now La Fabrica Central in Boston. It is there that she shares her beloved Caribbean cuisine—a multicultural fusion of flavors from Puerto Rico, Cuba, and the Dominican Republic.

The restaurant's name is a reference to the manufacture of rum on the islands. And of course, where there's rum, there's coquito. Toss aside any notion of eggnog as a creamy elixir relegated to the holidays alone; at La Fabrica, the iconic Puerto Rican milk punch is served every day in many variations. No matter the season or occasion, it's a spirited sip that exemplifies the notion that every day is meant to be celebrated, as Giovanna learned from the very start.

450 Massachusetts Avenue
Cambridge, MA 02139
857.706.1125
lafabricacentral.com

Coquito

America and Europe have eggnog, Venezuela has ponche crema, and Mexico has its rompope made with almond milk, yet many swear that once you've sipped a good Puerto Rican coquito, you won't be tempted by any of the others. Giovanna prefers Coco López or Goya brands of coconut cream in her recipes.

3 egg yolks	1 (8½-ounce) can
1 cup of white rum	coconut cream
¼ cup brandy or	(Coco López or
spiced rum	Goya)
1 (14-ounce) can	2 teaspoons
sweetened	ground
condensed milk	cinnamon
1 (12-ounce) can	2½ teaspoons
evaporated milk	vanilla extract

Combine the yolks with the liquor and process for 2 to 3 minutes. Blend in the rest of the ingredients and transfer to a clean glass bottle. Pour in an ice-filled rocks glass and garnish with a sprinkle of cinnamon and a cinnamon stick to serve. Refrigerate for up to 3 days.

VARIATIONS

Eggless Coquito: Combine 1½ cups white rum, 2 (13½-ounce) cans coconut milk, 1 (14-ounce) can sweetened condensed milk, 1 tablespoon vanilla extract, 1 cup coconut cream, 2 teaspoons ground cinnamon, and ¼ cup gold or brandy rum in a blender and process until well blended. Transfer to a clean glass bottle. Refrigerate. **Makes 8 cups.**

Chocolate Coquito: Combine 1½ cups white rum, 1 (13½-ounce) can coconut milk, 1 (14-ounce) can sweetened condensed milk, 1 (8½-ounce) can coconut cream, ½ cup chocolate syrup, and ½ cup Kahlua or brandy (or a mixture of both) in a blender and process until well blended. Transfer to a clean glass bottle. Refrigerate. **Makes 7 cups.**

Nutella Coquito: Combine 1 (8½-ounce) can coconut cream, 1 (14-ounce) can sweetened condensed milk, 1 (13½-ounce) can coconut milk, 1 (12-ounce) can evaporated milk, 1 cup Nutella, 1½ cups gold rum, 1 tablespoon vanilla extract, and 1 teaspoon ground cinnamon in a blender and process until well blended. Transfer to a clean glass bottle. Refrigerate. **Makes 7 cups.**

Pistacho Coquito: Combine 1 (8½-ounce) can coconut cream, 1 (14-ounce) can sweetened condensed milk, 1 (13½-ounce) can coconut milk, 2 cups pistachio ice cream, and 2 cups white rum in a blender and process until well blended. Transfer to a clean glass bottle. Refrigerate. **Makes 8½ cups.**

Spiced Rum Balls

A flavorful duo—spiced rum and pumpkin pie spice—add spirited flavor to this holiday favorite for giving and sharing, and definitely dunking. The variation shows how a few simple substitutions for the liquor, crumbs, and nuts takes this confection in a whole new direction.

¼ cup (2 ounces) spiced rum
3 tablespoons honey
½ teaspoon pumpkin pie spice
1 cup confectioners' sugar, plus more for rolling

2 cups finely crushed graham cracker crumbs (about 16 whole graham crackers)
1 cup finely chopped macadamia nuts

1. Stir together the rum and honey in a mixing bowl to combine. Gradually whisk the confectioners' sugar into the rum mixture until no lumps remain. Stir in the crumbs and nuts and with a wooden spoon until fully incorporated.

2. Compress heaping tablespoonfuls of the mixture in your palm and carefully form into balls about 1-inch in diameter. Roll some of the balls in a shallow dish of confectioners' sugar to evenly coat on all sides. Tap lightly to remove excess sugar. Store rum balls in an airtight container for up to 2 weeks.

VARIATION

Chocolate Bourbon Balls: Substitute bourbon for the spiced rum, Nabisco chocolate wafers (about 22 wafers) for the crumbs, and chopped pecans for the macadamia nuts. Roll these in cocoa powder instead of confectioners' sugar.

BRYANT'S COCKTAIL LOUNGE

There are creamy cocktails and then there are creamy classics like the Pink Squirrel, which is easily a day's sustenance in a single glass. The recipe for this spirited midcentury shake comes from the original source, the Milwaukee bar credited for introducing Wisconsin to the concept of the cocktail lounge. It's a wait-to-be-seated bar format with host, mood lighting, plush booths, and bar etiquette to rival Emily Post. Loudly croon or rudely cuss and you'll swiftly be shown the door.

First opened as a beer hall by Bryant Sharp in 1936, the place underwent a metamorphosis a few years later when he decided to trade in the jukebox for a hi-fi record player that spun only classical records and swap the steins of suds for fancy made-to-order cocktails. After a fire gutted the inside of the lounge in 1971, a new owner pulled out all the stops, renovating the interior with a three-tier rail, gold-plated cash registers, and fancy finishes at every turn. A menu full of ice cream cocktails, but also a lounge frozen in time, are reasons enough to stop in the next time you're in Milwaukee.

1579 S 9th Street
Milwaukee, WI 53204
414.383.2620
bryantscocktaillounge.com

SERVES 1

Pink Squirrel

Crème de noyaux tastes like almonds but is actually a rosy liqueur
made from the kernel inside the pits of stone fruits like apricots, peaches,
or cherries. You could substitute Amaretto in a pinch for its similar flavor
profile, but you'll end up with a muddy-brown Squirrel. A drop of red
food coloring or a splash of grenadine can bring the blush back. The
other key flavor that keeps the pink in the drink is the chocolate that
comes from clear crème de cacao. While at Bryant's, "Wisconsin"
ice cream is key; for the rest of us, your favorite vanilla will do.

2 ounces crème de noyaux
1 ounce light crème de cacao
2 scoops Wisconsin ice cream
(or 2 ounces heavy cream)

Lightly sweetened whipped
cream
Freshly grated nutmeg
Maraschino cherry

Blend the crème de noyaux, crème de cacao, and vanilla ice cream in
a blender until smooth and creamy. Pour into a pearl diver or other tall
glass and top with a spoonful of whipped cream, freshly grated nutmeg,
and a cherry.

WHAT'S IN A NAME?
The Pink Squirrel was named for its rosy
hue and nutty liqueur base (and perhaps
for the flush and squirrely feeling you get
after you've drunk a few).

Chocolate-Almond Cookies

Extra-dark chocolate and a healthy splash of chocolate liqueur give these chunky drop cookies rich, complex flavor. As for extract swaps, you could substitute the same amount of another complementary liqueur to change things up. Try Kahlua for a coffee note, kirsch for a hint of cherry, or Baileys Irish Cream for boozy richness.

½ cup (1 stick) unsalted butter, softened
1¼ cup packed dark brown sugar
1 large egg
1 tablespoon crème de cacao
1 teaspoon almond extract

1½ cups all-purpose flour
2 tablespoons extra-dark unsweetened cocoa powder
¼ teaspoon salt
1 cup chopped slivered almonds

1. Center racks in the oven and preheat to 300°F.

2. Combine the butter and dark brown sugar in a mixing bowl. Cream the ingredients with an electric mixer on medium speed until light and fluffy, about 3 minutes. Mix in the egg, crème de cacao, and almond extract and mix on high speed to incorporate. Stop to scrape down the sides of the bowl as necessary.

3. Whisk together the flour, cocoa powder, salt, and chopped almonds in a medium bowl. Gradually add the dry ingredients into the wet ingredients, stirring with a wooden spoon until combined. Drop level tablespoons of the mixture onto parchment-lined baking sheets, spacing about 2 inches apart. Flatten each with the bottom of a glass. Bake for 15 to 17 minutes, rotating the pans halfway through baking. Let cool on the pans for 3 minutes. Transfer the cookies to a rack to cool completely.

QUEEN'S PARK

Brooklyn bartender Laura Newman was searching for another city to open a bar when she took a detour to Birmingham to join her boyfriend. Little did she know that she'd fall for his hometown too. Soon she'd figured out that the "Magic City" was the place for the upscale watering hole focused on the classics she'd long dreamed about. She named it Queen's Park in honor of the Trinidad hotel that served as a spirited escape for Americans during Prohibition.

Her bar's signature cocktail, the Queen's Park Swizzle, was the namesake hotel's, too—dark rum, simple syrup, and lime juice, served with lots of crushed ice and a bouquet of fresh mint. The menu offers plenty of creamy classics, too, like the early-twentieth-century Batida, a Brazilian cachaça-based drink shaken with coconut, passion fruit, and lime. The Pisco Punch uses gomme (gum arabic), a flavorless pre-Prohibition bar staple, to bolster viscosity in a way sugar syrup cannot. Her Midori Sour surprisingly employs the traditional egg white for body in this age of vegan stand-ins.

In the dairy department, imbibers can sample a Ramos Gin Fizz, New Orleans Milk Punch, Grasshopper, bourbon-spiked Orange Julius, or the Dominicana, a deconstructed White Russian with rum, banana liqueur, coffee, and a sweetened cream float.

If all these options seem like overload, reconsider the enthusiasm of the source. After graduating from Connecticut College, Laura's journey to bartender began with an office job at a boutique liquor company, followed by hospitality management school, and a six-year stint working for a group that managed some of New York's most notable bars. She was hooked on the industry, yet found working behind the bar her true calling.

Laura's fascination with the provenance of classic cocktails is reflected in the history of each shared on her menu. Watching her work is pure theater. She moves quickly and effortlessly, mixing multiple drinks while conversing with patrons without missing a beat. She is the best bartender in America, after all. Last year Laura was the first woman to win the U.S. Bartenders' Guild World Class Competition. I consider her the queen!

112 24th Street North
Birmingham, AL 35203
queensparkbham.com

Midnight Breakfast

This sweet drink will transport you to childhood. It's liquid whimsy served in a mini milk bottle, beware! This one is hard to sip slowly.

1½ ounces Tito's vodka
.375 ounce (2¼ teaspoons) Vanilla Syrup (*recipe follows*)

4 ounces Fruity Pebbles Cereal Milk (*recipe follows*)
Handful of Fruity Pebbles, for garnish

Combine the vodka, vanilla syrup, and Fruity Pebbles cereal milk in an ice-filled shaker. Shake vigorously. Strain into a mini milk bottle or rocks glass. Garnish with Fruity Pebbles cereal. Serve with a straw.

Vanilla Syrup: Combine 1 cup granulated sugar with 1 cup water in a saucepan. Cut a vanilla bean pod in half lengthwise and scrape out the seeds with the tip of a knife. Add seeds and pod to saucepan. Bring the mixture to a simmer over medium-high heat. Stir until the sugar is completely dissolved. Remove from the heat and let sit, covered, for at least 1 hour. Strain through a fine-mesh strainer to remove pod and any other particles (vanilla seeds are okay). Transfer to a container and refrigerate for up to 1 month.

Cereal Milk: Combine 1½ quarts whole milk, 4 cups Fruity Pebbles cereal, ½ cup light brown sugar, and ½ teaspoon salt in a large vessel; stir thoroughly. Let sit 30 minutes, stirring every 5 to 10 minutes to ensure the sugar is dissolved. Fine strain and refrigerate. (Be sure to label with expiration date from milk container.)

WHAT'S IN A NAME?
This one is less about a midnight snack and everything about the final round. Cereal milk makes it breakfast-y, but booze makes it anything but (at least for most of us).

Brown Butter Cinnamon "Toasts"

This spin on breakfast toast is less sweet than your usual krispie treat. Browning butter adds nuttiness, while the ping of salt rounds out the flavor in this apropos cereal sidekick to accompany Laura Newman's playful Midnight Breakfast. If you have time, consider roasting the mini marshmallows under a broiler until they develop a brown char on the surface before adding them to the brown butter. The end result will have a rich, fireside s'mores flavor.

1 cup (2 sticks) good-quality salted butter, cut into pieces
¼ teaspoon kosher salt
1 (16-ounce) bag mini marshmallows

1 (12-ounce) box crisp rice cereal
2 tablespoons ground cinnamon

1. Grease a rimmed baking sheet and set aside.

2. Combine the butter and salt in a large stockpot or Dutch oven with a light-colored bottom and place over medium heat. Whisk the butter as it melts. Watch closely, as it will foam and then clear as the milk solids fall to the bottom of the pan and begin to turn golden brown. As soon as it begins to turn darker and you smell a nutty aroma, add the marshmallows to the pot and remove the pot from the heat. Stir until the marshmallows are melted and smooth. Fold in the cereal.

3. Turn the mixture out onto the prepared pan and press the mixture into an even layer with clean, greased palms. Sprinkle the surface with cinnamon. Let cool completely. Cut into triangles or "toast points" to serve.

EMPIRE STATE SOUTH

Amid the traffic and bustle of downtown Atlanta, a swath of greenspace is sandwiched by skyscrapers. The first floor of one of the buildings opens to a patio dotted with outdoor tables, Adirondack chairs, and a bocce court. At times the swath of grass feels like the lawn at a church picnic, this being the South and all. Inside, the menu features star chef Hugh Acheson's reinterpretation of Southern classics. Pickled shrimp mingle with blood orange and fennel, pork belly finds a complementary sidekick in kimchi, and collards come sauced with black vinegar and tangled up in toothsome grains.

Cocktails riff off classics too. Bar director Kellie Thorn says it's a great time to be in the drink-making business because customers are more interested than ever. She hopes people move beyond "I only drink bourbon" to focus on desired flavors instead. You don't eat the same dish at every meal, so why stick to the same liquor, she wonders. But she also admits that her craft is about great service, and there is no place for bartender ego. "If you don't care for the creations printed and want a Mojito or Cosmopolitan, I am happy to oblige," Kellie says.

The bar philosophy cultivated at Empire State South is complexity through simplicity. Too many ingredients muddle a drink and make it too time-consuming and costly to prepare. So Kellie always considers what might be subtracted and still maintain the desired result. Kellie's cocktail education may have been built on the classics—formulas she relies on today—but she can't help but go off the rails, too. She's been fat washing spirits with housemade orgeat, an almond syrup that's a mainstay in the bartender toolbox, and she loves an old-school clarified milk punch. No matter how time-consuming, she says that one's worth the effort. Though I think that her pistachio, pisco, and floral-meets-spice Plus One truly takes the cake.

999 Peachtree Street
Atlanta, GA 30309
404.541.1105
empirestatesouth.com

SERVES 1

Plus One

The cocktail was inspired by the flavors of the classic Persian Love Cake. Kellie uses Macchu Pisco here. Good-quality pisco is key.

2 ounces pisco
2 ounces Pistachio Milk
  (*recipe follows*)
¾ ounce Vanilla Syrup
  (page 93, but using
  2 vanilla beans)

¼ ounce fresh lime juice
1 dash Scrappy's Cardamom
  Bitters
2 dashes The Bitter Truth
  Rose Water
Freshly grated cinnamon

Combine all ingredients except the cinnamon with ice in a shaker tin and shake. Strain over fresh ice in a Collins glass or tall glass. Grate the cinnamon over the top.

Pistachio Milk: Soak 1 cup pistachios in 3 cups filtered water overnight. The next day, blend well in a blender. Strain the mixture through a nut-milk bag to remove solids. **Makes about 3 cups.**

WHAT'S IN A NAME?
"Love Cake" may be the jumping off point for the flavor of the cocktail, but its name is inspired by the date you bring to a friend's wedding: your "Plus One."

Peach-Spice Cookies

If you've ever had a muffintop (and no, not the one that hangs over your waistband) from the bakery, these cookies are very similar in looks and texture to the part of the muffin that spills over the paper liner. Moist, rich, and cakey, these cookies are about flavor over form. Georgia is the Peach State and, lord knows, every street in Atlanta has the word "Peach" in it, so peaches simply had to figure into a Plus One pairing. Fragrant stone fruit provides the perfect complement for the aromatic rose water and cardamom bitters in the pisco-spiked cocktail.

2 cups all-purpose flour
1 teaspoon baking soda
½ teaspoon salt
1 teaspoon ground cinnamon
1 teaspoon ground cardamom
½ teaspoon ground nutmeg

⅔ cup (10 tablespoons) unsalted butter, softened
1 cup granulated sugar
2 large eggs
8 ounces frozen peaches, pureed (about ¾ cup)
1 cup golden raisins

1. Preheat the oven to 375°F.

2. Whisk together the flour, baking soda, salt, cinnamon, cardamom, and nutmeg in a medium bowl.

3. Combine the butter and sugar in the bowl of a stand mixer fitted with the paddle attachment, starting on low speed. Cream the mixture by gradually increasing the speed to high until the mixture is light and fluffy, about 3 minutes. Beat in the eggs one at a time. Gradually beat in the flour mixture. Add the pureed peaches and raisins and beat to incorporate.

4. Drop rounded tablespoonfuls of dough onto two parchment-lined baking sheets, spacing about 1 inch apart. Bake for 12 minutes, or until the cookies are browned at the edges and set in the middle. Let cool on the pans 3 minutes. Transfer the cookies to a rack to cool completely. Store in an airtight tin at room temperatures for up to 3 days.

DOVE'S LUNCHEONETTE

In a 140-year-old building in Chicago's Wicker Park that once housed an Italian sandwich-and-coffee shop called Cipollina, a retro-style diner is hopping. The best seats in the house are all the same—forty-one swiveling diner stools bolted to a penny-tile floor in front of steel counters that flank walls, windows, and bar. This is Dove's Luncheonette, and you want to be here. Named for the character Dove Linkhorn in author Nelson Algren's novel *A Walk on the Wild Side*, Dove's serves breakfast, lunch, and dinner. The atmosphere is eye-catching Diner-Americana at every turn, but the elevated Mexican menu is unexpected.

Here Bartender Sam Carlton runs a notable agave spirits bar program. "The revival of the craft cocktail, and the subsequent spirits boom, came more or less hand in hand with the farm-to-table movement," Sam explains. He admits that bartenders are just beginning to get the attention that chefs and kitchens long have. "Bartenders across the world work very hard to self-educate, and put countless hours into research and development, as well as prep, in order to make what are very involved drinks look completely effortless. Many times that works too well, and the work behind the drink becomes invisible."

It's hard not to notice the creativity that goes into the cocktail menu at Dove's. The milk stout float was Sam's attempt to fulfill customer expectations of traditional diner offerings, but then subvert those expectations by bringing something alcoholic to the picture. It's whimsy that works, and it's not the only creamy cocktail that makes an appearance. "We frequently feature an egg-white drink. Something about its velvety texture is comforting, which is the feeling we want to evoke." In recent rotation was a Toasted Amaranth Horchata that Sam says was like cereal milk, only better. "The best drinks are simple and do more than taste good. They comfort, evoking memories and emotions," Sam believes. From design to drinks to dishes, Dove's nails nostalgia.

1545 N. Damen Avenue
Chicago, IL 60622
773.645.4060
doveschicago.com

Honeyed Vanilla Milk Stout Float

The team at Dove's uses housemade honeyed vanilla ice cream in this boozy spin on a root beer float. Replicate it by stirring ½ cup honey into a half gallon of softened vanilla ice cream, and then refreeze.

2 scoops Honeyed Vanilla Ice Cream
8 ounces chilled Left Hand Milk Stout (or any stout beer)

Dollop of whipped cream
Handful of Candied Spiced Almonds (*recipe follows*)

Put 2 scoops of the ice cream in a parfait glass and top with the stout beer. Garnish with a dollop of whipped cream and a sprinkling of candied almonds.

Candied Spiced Almonds

1 cup almonds
1 cup granulated sugar
1 tablespoon water

1 teaspoon cinnamon
Pinch of kosher salt

1. Preheat the oven to 300°F. Toast the almonds in a single layer on a sheet pan for 15 to 20 minutes.

2. Bring the sugar and water to a boil in a saucepan. Stir until the sugar is dissolved. Add the almonds and cinnamon. Reduce the heat to medium-low, stirring constantly until the sugar recrystallizes.

3. Transfer the nuts to a sheet pan, sprinkle with a pinch of salt, and let cool completely. Store in an airtight container at room temperature for up to 1 week. **Makes 1 cup.**

Dark Chocolate–Covered Potato Chips

Relying on that same nostalgia that Dove's bartender Sam Carlton does in his mixology, salty potato chips with a lunch counter ice cream float seems perfectly fitting. Dipped in dark chocolate, they taste otherworldly.

2 (3-ounce) dark-chocolate bars, chopped

5 ounces potato chips with ridges
Maldon sea salt flakes

1. Melt chocolate in a microwave-safe bowl for 1 to 1½ minutes, stopping to stir every 30 seconds, just until melted.

2. Dip the chips in the chocolate and place in a single layer on wax paper. Sprinkle with salt and allow the chocolate to dry completely.

3. Store the chips in an airtight container at room temperature for up to 1 day.

JUNOON

Passion is what made Junoon a Michelin-starred restaurant soon after opening its doors in 2010 and every year since, and "passion" is the meaning of the Hindi word that is the restaurant's name. Here, the kitchen team turns out innovative dishes that celebrate the enduring traditions and the regional foods of India, while pushing the cuisine forward with modern reinterpretations of classics using only the finest of ingredients and vibrant flavors.

Created to similarly entice and awe, the bar program focuses on spice-inspired mixology. "All our creations have to have some Asian ingredients including herbs, teas, and spices. This way we offer some new flavors to our guests and a cocktail that goes well with the food," explains bar manager Hemant Pathak. Interaction with the kitchen and pastry chefs, as well as a laser focus on seasonality, drives the cocktail menu. Hemant also keeps a finger on the pulse of what's happening in mixology on the global stage and experiments a lot. "Experimentation, when accepted, prompts creativity, and the Indian palate has always been spice-driven . . . and we all know that history of spices. For centuries, foreign traders came to India just to get access. Ha! They even colonized us for [spices]."

The bar's *Game of Thrones*–inspired menu plays with spices by focusing on a theme. Hemant admits that he had no idea what the show was even about five years ago, but once he did, he offered a King's Landing cocktail first. It really caught the attention of patrons. More GOT-inspired cocktails followed. Hemant says that he does his best to use spices as a way to express the character or place for which a drink is named. His warm Winter is Coming cocktail exemplifies Hemant's passion for his craft and the spice-inspired cocktail philosophy he so deftly and deliciously cultivates.

27 W 24th Street
New York, NY 10010
212.490.2100
junoonnyc.com

Winter Is Coming

Bartender Hemant Pathak creates bold, inventive cocktails to match Junoon's award-winning menu. This *Game of Thrones*–inspired cocktail came about on his quest to make a "bartender's soup" spiked with booze. He gets many requests for hot drinks during winter in the Big Apple, so he's always dreaming up uncommon creations. "I use Laird's Applejack as a base spirit during colder months and I couldn't think of anything better to blend it with than butternut squash." This vegetable-based cocktail is like a hot, winter rival to another vegetable-in-a-glass cocktail, the Bloody Mary.

1½ ounces Laird's
  Applejack
½ ounce coconut
  liqueur

4 ounces Hemant's
  Butternut Squash
  Soup (*recipe
  follows*)
Chili oil and
  pansy blossoms,
  for garnish

Slightly warm the Applejack, coconut liqueur, and soup in a saucepan and pour into a warm teacup. Garnish with drops of chili oil and pansy blossoms.

Hemant's Butternut Squash Soup

1 medium butternut
  squash, peeled
  and diced
4 star anise
3 sticks cinnamon
1¾ cups orange
  juice
3 whole cloves

3 whole allspice
1 teaspoon
  coriander seeds
2 cups coconut milk
8 pinches salt
6 to 8 teaspoons
  honey

1. Clip a candy or deep-frying thermometer to the side of a water-filled stockpot. Heat over medium–high until the water reaches 165°F.

2. Place the squash, star anise, and 2 cinnamon sticks in a large resealable bag. Remove excess air and seal. Clip the top of the bag to the side of the pot so the ingredients are submerged. Maintain a temperature of 165°F for 30 minutes. Alternatively, place the bag in a 165°F sous vide for 30 minutes. Remove the spices from the bag. Puree the squash in a high-speed blender.

3. Place the orange juice, remaining cinnamon stick, cloves, allspice, and coriander seeds in a saucepan over medium heat. Simmer until reduced by half. Remove from the heat and strain.

4. Add the squash puree to the saucepan over low heat. Stir in the coconut milk and the spiced orange juice. Add the salt and honey. Serve immediately or let cool, cover, and refrigerate. Reheat to serve.
Makes about 5 cups.

Benne Wafers

A Deep South staple, these crisp sesame wafers are light, crisp, and perfect for cocktail hour. I won't lie, this is perhaps my favorite "cookie" recipe in the entire book. Try to eat just one. Incorporating tahini, the nutty sesame seed butter, really ups the sesame flavor ante here.

½ cup all-purpose flour
¼ teaspoon kosher salt
⅛ teaspoon baking soda
¼ cup (½ stick) butter, softened
1 cup packed dark brown
  sugar

1 large egg
1 tablespoon tahini
½ cup toasted and cooled
  golden sesame seeds
½ cup toasted and cooled black
  sesame seeds

1. Center racks in the oven and preheat to 350°F.

2. Combine the flour, salt, and baking soda in a bowl and set aside. Cream the butter and brown sugar with a mixer at medium speed until light and fluffy, about 1 minute. Add the egg and tahini and beat until well blended. Stir in the dry ingredients and sesame seeds until evenly incorporated.

3. Drop by level tablespoons onto three parchment-lined 13 x 18-inch half sheet pans, spacing about 2 inches apart. Bake, in batches, for 8 to 10 minutes until golden. Transfer the wafers to a rack to cool completely. Let cool on the sheet pans for 2 minutes. Store in an airtight container until ready to serve.

TOSCA CAFE

The famed Tosca Cafe in San Francisco's North Beach welcomed new Glory Days after longtime owner, Jeanette Etheridge, passed the torch of her beloved saloon when faced with the prospect of having to close its doors. Actor Sean Penn, a regular in Tosca's exclusive Back Room, reached out to New York friends Ken Friedman and Chef April Bloomfield of the award-winning Spotted Pig for help to keep Tosca ticking. The two accepted the challenge and breathed new life into the beloved late-night watering hole and after-shift hangout for restaurant-industry professionals. The new owners also re-opened the kitchen, making Tosca Cafe a destination for an incomparable meal, too.

Originally opened by three Italians who came to San Francisco after World War I in 1919, Tosca was named after one of their daughters. As bad luck would have it, Prohibition became the law of the land only a few weeks after opening, potentially dooming the business. The industrious partners hatched a plan: One headed to Sonoma County to make bootleg brandy while the other two installed giant espresso machines from Italy at either end of the bar. Tosca was now officially a café, allowing them to fly beneath the radar (or the equivalent of a radar in 1919) of the law, even though Tosca cappuccinos came spiked with that Sonoma County bootlegged brandy.

Bar director Nick Stolte explains that while customers could order a regular coffee or cappuccino at the original Tosca, there never was actual coffee in the House Cappuccino. It was always code for brandy-spiked hot chocolate. Today, bartenders will make a "dirty" house cappuccino upon request, which is this same recipe with a shot of espresso mixed in with the chocolate.

242 Columbus Avenue
San Francisco, CA 94133
415.986.9651
toscacafesf.com

Tosca's House "Cappuccino" 1919

This cocktail has seen many iterations over the years, but bar director Nick Stolte believes this current cappuccino is the café's finest. It pays homage to the original by using a California brandy and uses a quality locally produced chocolate in the rich housemade ganache. The ganache and vanilla syrup are both delicious stirred into strong coffee for a rich mocha or into steamed milk for an "unspiked" hot chocolate.

1 ounce Bertoux California brandy

4 ounces hot Tosca House Cappuccino Mix (*recipe follows*)
Steamed milk

Pour the brandy into the bottom of a warm 6-ounce Irish coffee mug. Top with the hot Tosca house cappuccino mix. Spoon steamed milk on top to the rim of the glass. Serve hot.

Tosca House Cappuccino Mix

8 ounces (1 cup) dandelion chocolate ganache (*recipe follows*)

4 ounces (½ cup) organic whole milk

1 ounces (2 tablespoons) vanilla syrup (*recipe follows*)

Whisk everything together in a large saucepan over medium-low heat until hot, being careful not to burn. Refrigerate leftovers and use within 3 days. **Makes about 1⅔ cups (or enough for about 3 drinks).**

Dandelion Chocolate Ganache

11 ounces (1¼ cup plus 2 tablespoons) organic heavy cream

5½ ounces Dandelion dark chocolate

¾ teaspoons kosher salt

Whisk cream and chocolate over medium heat just until the chocolate is melted into cream. It doesn't need much heat, so be careful that you do not cook the cream. Add the salt. Refrigerate any leftovers for up to 3 days. **Makes about 2½ cups.**

Vanilla Syrup

½ cup (4 ounces) organic cane sugar

½ cup (4 ounces) water

½ fresh vanilla bean

Heat the sugar and water until the sugar is dissolved, but do not reduce. Split the vanilla bean and scrape the halves with the tip of a spoon. Stir the vanilla bean halves and bean residue into the warm syrup. Let the syrup sit for at least 24 hours; strain before using. **Makes 1 cup.**

Chocolate-Dipped Hazelnut Shortbread

These are decadent and delicious with a steaming nightcap or coffee.

½ cup hazelnuts
½ cup (1 stick) butter, softened
½ cup granulated sugar
½ teaspoon vanilla extract
1 cup all-purpose flour

Pinch kosher salt
One 4-ounce semisweet
(60% cocoa) baking bar,
chopped

1. Center racks in the oven and preheat to 350°F.

2. Arrange the hazelnuts on a baking sheet. Bake for 10 minutes until toasted. Wrap the nuts in a clean kitchen towel; let stand for 2 minutes. Rub gently to loosen the skins, let cool and finely chop. Set aside ¼ cup of the chopped nuts to garnish after dipping in the chocolate.

3. Beat the butter with an electric mixer for 2 minutes. Gradually add the sugar and beat on medium speed until creamy, about 3 minutes. Add the vanilla. Stop to scrape down the sides of the bowls as necessary.

4. Whisk together the flour and salt. Gradually add with ¼ cup chopped hazelnuts to the wet ingredients, beating on low speed until combined. Halve the dough and shape into two logs about 8 inches long and 2 inches in diameter. Wrap in plastic wrap and chill for at least 2 hours.

5. Preheat the oven to 350°F.

6. Slice one chilled log into ¼-inch slices. Arrange 2 inches apart on 2 parchment-lined baking sheets. Bake 12 to 15 minutes, or until golden. Cool on the pans for 5 minutes then on a rack to cool completely.

7. Microwave the chopped chocolate on high for about 1½ minutes, or until melted, stopping to stir several times. Dip each cooled cookie in the melted chocolate, allowing any excess to drip back in the bowl. Place the dipped cookies on a sheet of parchment and sprinkle them with the reserved chopped hazelnuts before the chocolate sets.

CHAPTER 3

THE

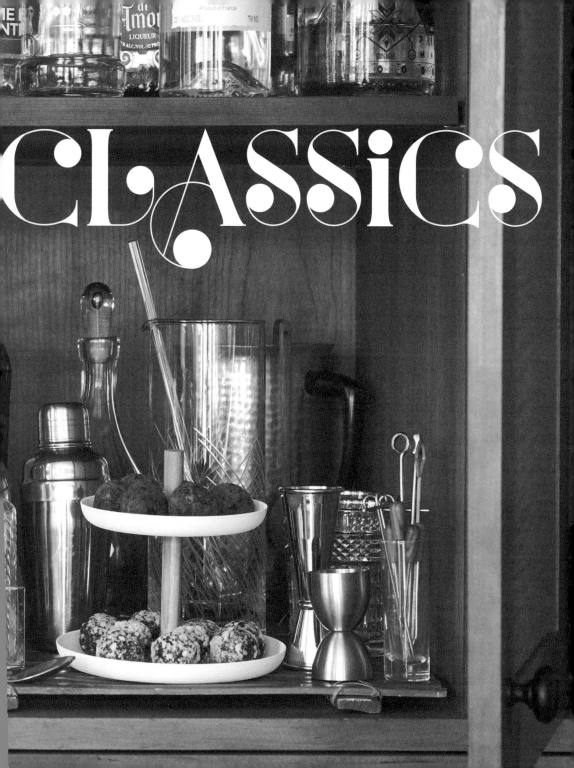

CLASSICS

GIN

The woodsy, resinous flavor of gin comes from juniper berries. The English spirit evolved from the medicinal Dutch *jenever*, a malt wine distillation that used juniper berries and herbs to mask the spirit's harsh flavors and make the finished product more palatable and interesting. Grain-based gins rose in popularity in England in the mid-1600s as the base spirit for many liqueurs, including fruit-infused Sloe Gin.

When buying gin, know that bottles labeled simply "Gin" refer to a neutral base spirit that has been flavored with juniper and other ingredients after distillation. It is considered the lowest quality.

Better-quality "Distilled Gin" refers to liquor that actually has been distilled with juniper berries and botanicals, though the spirit may be further blended with flavorings or sweeteners after distillation. Top-quality "London Dry" gin is all-natural, with no additional flavors or colors added after distillation. Though most often served on the rocks with tonic, gin features prominently in a handful of luxuriously rich cocktail like sours, notably the Ramos Gin Fizz, as well as rich and sweet after-dinner drinks like the creamy Ace. Worth noting, long before brandy or bourbon, gin was the spirit of choice in the original Alexander.

Ramos Gin Fizz

It made no difference that the preparation of his namesake cocktail was a heavy lift, Henry Ramos was a perfectionist behind the bar. He was also a dedicated family man who closed his bar at eight o'clock to spend evenings at home, where he believed his customers should be as well. When Prohibition began, he shuttered his bar for good and submitted his famous gin fizz recipe to the *Times Picayune* for publication. This is it.

1½ ounces London Dry gin	2 drops vanilla extract
½ ounce fresh lemon juice	2 ounces heavy cream
½ ounce fresh lime juice	1 fresh egg white
1 ounce simple syrup	Club soda
2 drops orange flower water	1 lime zest curl

Combine all the ingredients, except the club soda, in a shaker tin. Dry shake without ice for 30 seconds to emulsify the cream and egg white. Add ice to the shaker. Shake vigorously for 3 to 4 minutes. Strain into a chilled fizz glass or Collins glass and top with soda until the raft of foam rises about 1 inch above the rim. Garnish with a lime zest curl.

Pairing: Lemon-Lavender Icebox Cookies, page 9

Ace

Like the blushing Shirley Temple, the Ace gets its rosy hue from grenadine. Make your own to avoid red dyes, fillers, and corn syrup. It keeps for several weeks in the refrigerator.

1 ounce gin	½ ounce heavy
½ ounce	cream
Pomegranate	1 egg white
Syrup (recipe	Juice of ½ lemon
follows) or	Freshly grated
grenadine	nutmeg

Combine all the ingredients in a shaker tin. Dry shake for 30 seconds. Add ice to the shaker and shake vigorously for 1 minute until the egg white and cream are emulsified and the drink is chilled. Strain into a chilled coupe glass and garnish with a grating of nutmeg.

Pomegranate (Grenadine) Syrup:

Combine 1 cup granulated sugar, ⅛ teaspoon salt, and 1 cup pomegranate juice in a saucepan over medium heat. Bring to a simmer, stirring often until the sugar dissolves. Remove from the heat. Add ¼ teaspoon orange flower water. **Makes about 1 cup.**

Pairing: White Chocolate-Cherry-Pistachio Oatmeal Cookies, page 55

Original Alexander

Also called a Whiteout, this is how the Alexander, now commonly made with brandy, was first served. Of course, you may swap the gin for brandy if you prefer, or keep the gin and use crème de banane instead of crème de cacao for a Silver Jubilee.

2 ounces gin	¾ ounce crème de
1 ounce heavy	cacao
cream	Freshly grated
	nutmeg

Combine the gin, cream, and crème de cacao in an ice-filled shaker tin. Shake vigorously for 10 to 12 seconds. Strain into a brandy snifter and garnish with a grating or two of nutmeg.

Pairing: Chocolate-Almond Cookies, page 71

VODKA

The name vodka is derived from the Russian word *voda*, or water, and was thought to first have been produced by monks in Russia from an imported base spirit and cereal grains rather than potatoes, as often touted. However, Poland also takes credit as the originator of the world's bestselling liquor. While vodka *may* be made from potatoes, it is most commonly made from wheat or rye, but also corn, sugar beets, vegetables, or many other fermentable ingredients.

After fermentation with alcohol and water, additions of sugar or sodium bicarbonate are sometimes added to soften the spirit's bite. Vodka is also occasionally filtered through charcoal to render it as neutral in flavor as possible. In the United States, it is the most popular liquor used in mixed drinks. It's the reigning spirit in Russia, where it is most often drunk straight.

The neutrality of vodka lets other flavors shine in cocktails, and creamy ones are no exception. From the ubiquitous White Russian to the luscious Mudslide, vodka is often barely noticed until its presence sneaks up on you.

White Russian

The midcentury Black Russian became the White Russian with the addition of cream. It's a drink that actor Jeff Bridges' character, The Dude, in *The Big Lebowski* put back in the spotlight twenty-plus years ago. If you trade the vodka for scotch, call it a Sneaky Peat (or Pete, which is a reference to a sneaky character).

2 ounces vodka　　**Heavy cream**
1 ounce Kahlua

Stir the vodka and Kahlua together in an ice-filled rocks glass. Top off with a splash of heavy cream. Stir and serve.

Pairing: Buttery Tuiles with Irish Cream Filling, page 59

VARIATION
Brave Bull: Substitute tequila for the vodka and shake in an ice-filled shaker tin. Strain into a coupe glass and garnish with a dollop of whipped cream.

Mudslide

Often served as a boozy milkshake, the spirited flavors of this retro cocktail are best experienced when the drink is blended with ice.

1 ounce vodka　　**1 ounce heavy**
1 ounce coffee　　**　cream**
**　liqueur**　　　　**Drizzle of**
1 ounce Irish cream　**　chocolate syrup**
**　liqueur**　　　　**　(optional)**

Blend the vodka, liqueurs, cream, and a handful of ice in a high-speed blender on high until frothy and combined. Pour into a coupe and drizzle a bit of chocolate syrup on top, if desired.

Pairing: Chocolate-Dipped Hazelnut Shortbread, page 95

Dreamsicle

This playful cocktail is reminiscent of the ice cream truck push-up pop favorite. For a less sweet drink, use orange seltzer.

2 ounces whipped cream vodka
1 ounce orange liqueur
4 ounces heavy cream

Orange soda or orange seltzer
1 orange slice

Combine the vodka, orange liqueur, and cream in an ice-filled shaker. Shake vigorously for 12 seconds, then strain into an ice-filled Collins glass. Top with orange soda or orange seltzer and stir with a bar spoon. Garnish with an orange slice.

Pairing: Five-Spice Gingersnaps, page 46

RUM

A close second to vodka in worldwide popularity, rum is a distillate of molasses from sugarcane production that was originally produced in the Caribbean but is now produced around the globe. Countries differ on the standards that must be met in its manufacture—maturation time, alcohol percentage, additives, and flavorings.

The varieties of rum are many, but the most popular Caribbean rums are from Puerto Rico, Cuba, and the Dominican Republic, and are distilled for the shortest amount of time. Labeled "light" or "white," they are mild and sweet in flavor. Stronger, aged rums from former British colonies are gold to amber and more complex in flavor, while full-bodied black rums are aged in charred barrels. Navy rum refers to the style of dark rum made from demerara sugar that was once provided as a daily ration to the British navy. Overproof rum refers to a product that is more than 100 proof. Gaining in popularity, young, mild rhum agricole—such as the Clement Canne Bleu rum that is blended with four other rum varieties in Here Nor There's Milk & Honey (page 8)—hails from French-speaking Caribbean colonies and is made from the fresh-pressed juices of a single variety of sugarcane rather than molasses.

As you might expect, rum works beautifully in creamy drinks on its own or blended with other spirits and liqueurs in tiki mixes, craft cocktails, or hot tipples whether the base is coconut milk, nut milk, or dairy.

Hot Buttered Rum

As the name suggests, this hot toddy gets its rich, creamy body from a grating of fresh, cold butter on top. As it melts, it floats on top and the drinker gets a bit of buttery richness with each soul-warming sip.

1 demerara (raw) sugar cube	Ice-cold butter
2 ounces dark rum	Pinch ground cinnamon
Boiling water	1 cinnamon stick

Heat an Irish coffee mug with boiling water. Dump out the water and place the sugar cube in the bottom of the warm glass. Grind it with a muddler or the back of a spoon. Add the rum and top with boiling water. Grate about 1 tablespoon cold butter on top, sprinkle with cinnamon, and serve with a cinnamon stick.

Pairing: Benne Wafers, page 88

Hummer Cocktail

This classic was created by Jerome Adams of Detroit's Bayview Yacht Club in the late 60s. It's an ice cream social in a glass. You can also substitute cream and ice for the ice cream for a similar result.

1½ ounces white rum	2 scoops vanilla ice cream
1½ ounces coffee liqueur	3 ice cubes

Place all the ingredients in a blender and blend until frothy and combined. Pour into a rocks glass.

Pairing: Spiced Rum Balls, page 66

WHAT'S IN A NAME?
It's said that the drink got its name when Jerome poured his experimental batch for the club's chairman and two friends who'd walked in after a hockey game and wanted to sample whatever he was making. After each man had sucked down two drinks, one guy said, "It kinda makes you wanna hum," and the Hummer was born.

Piña Colada

The national drink of Puerto Rico was the star of Don the Beachcomber's tiki drink craze. It's become a beach-vacationer favorite around the globe.

4 ounces fresh pineapple juice
1 ounce white rum
1 ounce gold rum

2 ounces cream of coconut
1 Maraschino cherry
1 pineapple wedge

Combine the juice, rums, and cream of coconut with 1 cup crushed ice in a blender. Blend until frothy. Pour into a hurricane glass and garnish with a cherry and wedge of pineapple.

Pairing: Coconut-Banana Macaroons, page 50

TEQUILA & MEZCAL

Tequila is mezcal, but not all mezcal is tequila. Tequila is a regional mezcal made in one of five states, but mostly in highland or lowland areas of Jalisco, solely from the blue Weber agave (or maguey plant). Tequila may be blended with other distillates, while smoky mezcal may be produced from several varieties of agave. Quality mezcals are primarily crafted in small batches by hand in one of eight states with most produced in the state of Oaxaca.

It takes over a decade for an agave to mature and send up a flower stalk. The flower stalk is cut, which causes juices to settle in the heart of the pineapple-like plant base or *piña*. Blades are used to remove the leaves, and then the hearts are taken to the distillery to be roasted to turn the starchy juices into sugar for distillation. Traditionally, agave for tequila are slow-roasted in brick ovens, while for mezcal they are roasted over wood in earthen pits, which gives the spirit its distinctive smoky flavor.

Both tequila and mezcal are traditionally sipped straight in Mexico, but as their popularity has soared beyond the country's borders, so have the many ways these spirits are being used in mixed drinks, including creamy concoctions.

Aztec Hot Chocolate

Drinks labeled "Aztec" include tequila or mezcal, of course, but often cinnamon, cocoa, or chiles—flavors synonymous with Latin cuisine.

1 cup whole milk
¼ cup heavy cream
2 tablespoons simple syrup
¼ cup extra-dark cocoa powder
½ teaspoon cinnamon
¼ teaspoon cayenne pepper
1½ ounces mezcal
Dollop of whipped cream
1 cinnamon stick

1. Heat the milk, cream, and simple syrup in a small saucepan over medium-high heat to a simmer, stirring occasionally. Remove from the heat.

2. Whisk together the cocoa powder, cinnamon, and cayenne in a heatproof cappuccino mug. Gradually whisk in the hot milk mixture to incorporate the cocoa and spices into the liquid and avoid lumps. Stir in the mezcal. Garnish with whipped cream and serve with a cinnamon stick.

Pairing: Brown Butter Cinnamon "Toasts," page 76

Montezuma

An adaptation of the drink that first appeared in the 1988 edition of *Mr. Boston: Official Bartender's Guide.*

1½ ounces añejo tequila
1 ounce Madeira
1 egg yolk

Place the tequila, Madeira, and egg yolk in a blender. Add ½ cup crushed ice. Blend on low speed until frothy and blended. Pour into a champagne flute to serve.

Pairing: Pepita Wedding Cookies, page 33

WHAT'S IN A NAME?
Blanco (white) tequila bottled soon after distillation has a less pronounced flavor than its aged counterparts.

Plata (silver) is clear like blanco, but aged for a few weeks.

Oro (gold) is blanco or plata tequila to which caramel color has been added.

Joven (young) blanco tequila blended with reposado for complexity.

Reposado (rested) rested for up to a year in wood barrels, which imparts a golden hue.

Añejo (aged) has rested up to three years. Lengthier aging equals mellower tequila.

Extra Añejo has rested over three years, which makes it dark and similar to brown liquors like bourbon and whiskey.

Cocorita

Never fear curdling here, this classic safely gets the creamy treatment. Unlike dairy, coconut milk won't turn to curds and whey when mixed with citrus and alcohol. Just an ounce of canned coconut milk lends flavor and body without heaviness.

1 tablespoon sweetened flaked coconut, toasted
1 tablespoon coarse salt
1 lime wedge
1½ ounces blanco tequila

1 ounce triple sec
1 ounce freshly squeezed lime juice
1 ounce canned coconut milk

1. Spread the coconut and salt in a single layer on a small plate. Rub a lime wedge around the rim of a 6-ounce margarita glass and save the wedge for garnish. Invert the glass on the plate and twist to coat the rim; reserve the remaining rim salt for a second round. Add ice to the glass.

2. Combine the tequila, triple sec, lime juice, and coconut milk in an ice-filled shaker tin. Cover and shake vigorously for 12 seconds. Strain in the prepared glass, garnish, and serve.

Pairing: Coconut-Banana Macaroons, page 50

WHISKEY

Lacking grapes to make wine, Christian monks in Scotland and Ireland began distilling barley in copper stills and then aging it in oak barrels as early as the eleventh century. The word "whiskey" comes from a Gaelic word that means "water of life." The spirit became so popular that King James IV of Scotland granted large stores of the country's malt to a friar to keep *aquavitae* (Latin for "water of life") flowing by order of the king.

After the formation of Great Britain in the 1700s, high taxes were levied on many goods, which forced distillers to move operations underground and make whiskey by the light of the moon. The word "moonshine" became an enduring nickname for bootlegged spirits. Whiskey became a form of currency during the Revolutionary War, and in the late 1700s, the first commercial distillery in America was founded in Louisville, Kentucky. Just like that, a burgeoning stateside whiskey industry was born.

Whether its whisky, whiskey, blended whiskey, Scotch, bourbon, rye, Tennessee, or Canadian, all whiskey is made from fermented grain mash.

The resulting spirit is versatile and delicious in rich cocktails like milk punch, sours, fizzes, or flips, and no coffee could be called Irish without it.

WHAT'S IN A NAME?

Scotch Scotch is whisky without an *e*, and single-malt Scotch must be made at a single distillery from a mash of peat-smoked malted barley in copper pot stills and aged in oak barrels. Most bottles of Scotch are a blend from several barrels and the age noted on a bottle refers to the youngest whisky in the blend.

Irish Made from kiln-dried, raw, and malted barley or other grains, Irish whiskey is triple-distilled and thus lighter in taste than Scotch. It must be made in the Republic of Ireland and aged for at least three years in wooden casks.

American American whiskeys are mostly bourbons made from fermented corn mash started by blending some mash from an older fermentation, or sour mash, into a new mash. Makers of Tennessee whiskey filter the spirit through maple charcoal, which they believe distinguishes their product from bourbon, which puts it in its own category.

Rye Liquor made from some fermented rye grains. It can be made from varying proportions with other grains such as barley and corn in Canada, where it is referred to as Canadian Whisky, and must be made with at 51% rye in America. Only one producer in Canada makes a spirit from 100% rye grain.

Derby Fizz

A fizz fit for the races, this sour has nice complexity with orange liqueur and a shot of rum.

2 ounces bourbon
1 ounce white rum
¼ ounce orange liqueur
1 ounce freshly squeezed lemon juice
1 ounce simple syrup
1 egg white
Club soda
1 orange wedge

Combine the bourbon, rum, orange liqueur, lemon juice, simple syrup, and egg white in an ice-filled shaker tin. Shake vigorously. Strain into a chilled highball glass and top with soda. Garnish with a wedge of orange.

Pairing: Tangerine Bars, page 19

Whiskey Sour

The formula for a classic punch is: one of sour, two of sweet, three of strong, four of weak. If you swap the ratio of sour for sweet, it is a flavorful formula for a sour cocktail. To match the formula's rhyme using a sour ratio, it would be two of sour, one of sweet, three of strong, four of weak.

2 ounces freshly squeezed lemon juice
1 ounce simple syrup
3 ounces bourbon
1 egg white
2 dashes Angostura bitters
1 Maraschino cherry

Combine the lemon juice, syrup, bourbon, and egg white in an ice-filled shaker tin. Shake vigorously. Strain into a chilled coupe. Garnish with two dashes bitters and a Maraschino cherry.

Pairing: Lemon-Lavender Icebox Cookies, page 9

Whiskey Flip

Thick, rich, and potent, flips use the whole egg instead of just the white for an uncommonly unctuous cocktail.

1 whole egg	**1 ounce rye**
½ teaspoon	**whiskey**
confectioners'	**Freshly grated**
sugar	**nutmeg**

Combine the egg, sugar, and rye in an ice-filled shaker tin. Shake vigorously. Strain into a sour or delmonico glass. Garnish with a grating or two of nutmeg. Serve immediately.

Pairing: Five-Spice Gingersnaps, page 46

Irish Coffee

Though this cocktail recipe is a basic you might find served at most any bar, it is elevated by its garnish. Bartender and Irishman Jim McCourt was kind enough to share the recipe for the savory topping he sprinkles on top of the Irish Coffees he serves at Prohibition in Charleston, South Carolina.

2 raw sugar cubes	**1 ounce heavy**
6 ounces strong	**cream**
piping-hot coffee	**Grán Rósta Powder**
1½ ounces Irish	**(optional; *recipe***
whiskey	***follows*)**

Place the sugar cubes in the bottom of an Irish coffee mug. Pour the hot coffee and Irish whiskey over the sugar. Float the cream over the back of a spoon to form a raft on top of the coffee. Garnish with the grán rósta powder. Serve immediately.

Jim McCourt's Prohibition (page 2) Grán Rósta Powder: In a blender or food processor, combine 1 cup of freshly popped salted and buttered popcorn with 1 cup of maltodextrin (available online or at vitamin stores). Blend until the mixture has the texture of fine sand. (The maltodextrin cuts the fat in the popcorn butter, so the resulting powder is not greasy.) Store in an airtight container up to several days.

Pairing: Benne Wafers, page 88

WHAT'S IN A NAME?
Grán rósta is the Irish word for popcorn.

NEW CREAM LIQUEUR

Cream liqueurs traditionally denote a product that has dairy cream suspended in a base spirit, with Baileys Irish Cream being the first in the category. The company successfully infused whiskey with dairy cream, producing a product with a two-and-a-half-year shelf life, whether refrigerated or not. With that, the popularity of cream liqueurs soared. Many companies followed suit–focusing on dairy-liquor spins and, more recently, spirited alternative-dairy milks made from seeds or nuts emulsified in a distilled liquor base.

While cream liqueurs often get a bad rap, they are a quick-and-easy way to mix up a rich cocktail without the need for a handful of mixers, syrups, or refrigerated add-ins. The cream liqueur category is constantly growing. From outliers like Licor 43 Orochata's tiger nut milk base to mainstream newcomers like Baileys Almande– classic Irish cream made from vegan almond milk–there is renewed interest in exploring this tasty trend.

Baileys Almande + Coconut Water Refresher

If a creamy cocktail could be dairy-free, gluten-free, and vegan all at once, this is it. Almond milk is the creamy star of the liqueur, but potassium-rich coconut water is the ideal mixer.

3 ounces Baileys Almande Almondmilk Liqueur

3 ounces coconut water

Pour the Baileys and coconut water over ice in a rocks glass. Stir with a bar spoon to combine. Serve immediately.

Pairing: Buttery Tuiles with Irish Cream Filling, page 58

Bom Bom Fully Baked Shakeawake

Bom Bom, which means "sweet sweet" in Portuguese, is a chocolate treat in Brazil, and refers to one's sweetheart in Spain, is also a liquor brand that describes itself as "the Ben & Jerry's of alcohol" while having 40% fewer calories and 40% less sugar than traditional cream liqueurs. The lineup includes creamy, dairy-based Nilli Vanilla and Coco Mochanut flavors, and alt-dairy Fully Baked (a wink-and-nod to its hemp seed milk base).

1 scoop Ben & Jerry's Half-Baked ice cream

2 ounces Bom Bom Fully Baked liqueur Double shot (4 ounces) brewed espresso

Combine the ice cream, liqueur, espresso, and a handful of ice in a high–speed blender. Blend on high until thick and smooth. Serve in a parfait glass with a straw and a spoon.

Pairing: Mint Chocolate Chip Cookies, page 63

Barraquito

Licor 43 Orochata blends the brand's signature golden (oro) liqueur made from citrus and fruit juices, spices, and vanilla with the classic dairy-free Spanish horchata made from pressed tigernuts. Delicious sipped over ice, it is also a key component of this layered cocktail that is a mainstay on the Canary Islands.

1 ounce sweetened condensed milk
2 ounces Licor 43 Orochata

Double shot (4 ounces) brewed espresso
Steamed milk
Ground cinnamon
1 lemon peel strip

Pour boiling water into a 10-ounce glass to warm it, and then empty the glass. Add the sweetened condensed milk to the bottom of the glass. Slowly pour the Licor 43 over the back of a spoon so that it floats on top of the condensed milk. Pour hot espresso over the back of the spoon so that it floats on top of the liqueur. Spoon steamed milk up to the rim of the glass. Sprinkle the surface of the drink with cinnamon and garnish with a lemon peel strip. Serve with a spoon and mix the layers together before drinking.

Pairing: Five-Spice Gingersnaps, page 46

Red Hotta RumChata

Though served on the rocks, this drink will warm you up from the inside out. It tastes like Red Hots candies melted into a boozy glass of milk. Manufactured in Wisconsin, RumChata is a cream liqueur made from Caribbean rum that has been distilled five times and blended with real dairy cream and infused with cinnamon, vanilla, and proprietary flavors.

1½ ounce RumChata

1½ ounce Fireball whiskey
Ground cinnamon
Cinnamon stick

Combine the RumChata and Fireball whiskey in an ice-filled rocks glass. Stir with a bar spoon. Garnish with a sprinkle of cinnamon and a cinnamon stick.

Pairing: Pepita Wedding Cookies, page 33

Sōmrus Pousse-Café

Though it hit the market in 2014, Sōmrus claims to be the "original Indian cream liqueur" with roots dating back to 2600 BC. Like its made-in-Wisconsin cousin, RumChata, rum is the base spirit for this liqueur, but its exotic flavor notes come from cardamom, saffron, and rose as well as pistachios and almonds. Try it in a layered shot, or as a pousse-café (literally "push coffee" in French), or chaser, that is drunk after coffee. This recipe is a spin on the classic B-52 shot using Sōmrus in place of the usual Irish cream.

½ **ounce Kahlua**
½ **ounce Sōmrus liqueur**

½ **ounce Cointreau triple sec**

Pour the Kahlua in the bottom of a shot glass. Slowly pour the Sōmrus over the back of a spoon to float on top of the Kahlua. Slowly pour the Cointreau over the back of the spoon to float on top of the Sōmrus. Do not stir. Enjoy in one gulp.

Pairing: Chocolate-Dipped Hazelnut Shortbread, page 95

WHAT'S IN A NAME?
Sōmrus means "nectar of the Gods" in Hindi.

Amarula Cream Don Pedro

SERVES 1

The Don Pedro was created in the 1970s by a South African restaurant owner who traveled to Scotland and poured his shot of Scotch over ice cream on a distillery tour and thought it delicious. Back at his restaurant, he added cream to make it sippable through a straw and it was a hit with diners. Often called a "Dom Pedro," the drink was not named for a clergyman. Here, ice cream is doused similarly, only with South African Amarula Cream in honor of the drink's South African inventor.

1 scoop vanilla ice cream
3 ounces Amarula Cream

½ cup half-and-half
Shaved chocolate

Blend the ice cream, Amarula Cream, and half-and-half in a high-speed blender on high until frothy and combined. Pour into a wineglass. Garnish with shaved chocolate. Serve with a straw.

Pairing: Tangerine Bars, page 19

WHAT'S IN A NAME?
Amarula Cream is made in South Africa from vitamin C-rich marula fruit. It tastes distinctively fruity.

BRANDY & FORTIFIED WINE

Brandy is a wine-based spirit, while fortified wine is a wine to which a distilled spirit, usually brandy, has been added. Fortified wines include Madeira, Marsala, vermouth, port, and sherry to name a few.

Brandy is made all over the world from the distilled pomace of young grapes. There are also fruit brandies, called *eau de vie* (French for "water of life"). Top-quality pomace brandies, such as French cognac and Armagnac, are aged in oak barrels, which lends to their rich, dark color. Lesser-quality brandies have coloring added to mimic the aged hue. Brandy is typically served in a small snifter glass that is easily warmed by hands to bring out the complexity of flavors.

From the quintessential Alexander to the Daisy, Sidecar, Fizz, and Flip, the versatility of fortified wines and brandy work surprisingly well in full-bodied cocktails.

WHAT'S IN A NAME?

Cognac is a carefully blended mix of brandies made from the grapes from six appellations or crus that radiate outward from the town of Cognac. French law allows cognac to be labeled with these designations:

VS (very superior) cognacs are blends of brandies aged for a minimum of 2 years. Wood chips are often soaked in these young cognacs to deepen the flavor. Additions of caramel color and sugar are almost guaranteed.

VSOP (very superior old pale) is a category that has been aged a minimum of 4½ years.

XO (extra old) the youngest cognac in the blend must be at least 6 years old, but it is not uncommon for 30- to 40-year-old brandy to be blended into cognac of this highest designation.

Tom & Jerry

This batter-topped cocktail is said to have been created by bartender Jerry Thomas at St. Louis's Planter House Hotel in the 1850s, though earlier references to a similar drink exist. Wherever it was born, it endures as a wintertime favorite.

1 ounce cognac or brandy	Hot whole milk
1 ounce dark rum	Grated fresh nutmeg
1 tablespoon Tom & Jerry batter (*recipe follows*)	Ground cloves

Fill an Irish coffee mug with boiling water to warm it. Discard the water. Add a spoon of batter to the bottom of the warm mug. Top with the brandy and rum. Slowly pour hot milk almost to the rim. Garnish with a grating of nutmeg and pinch of ground cloves.

Tom & Jerry Batter

2 eggs, separated	2 tablespoons confectioners' sugar
Pinch cream of tartar	2 teaspoons brandy

Whisk the eggs whites with a pinch of cream of tartar in a bowl until foamy. Add 1 tablespoon of the confectioners' sugar and whisk until you have soft peaks. Whisk the egg yolks in a separate bowl until smooth. Whisk in the remaining tablespoon confectioners' sugar and the brandy. Gently fold the egg whites into the yolks and refrigerate the mixture until ready to use. **Makes batter for about 6 drinks.**

Pairing: Spiced Rum Balls, page 66

Arago

Cognac is the spirited player in this creamy cocktail spiked with banana liqueur.

1½ ounce cognac	1 ounce heavy cream
1½ ounce crème de banane	

Combine the cognac, banana liqueur, and cream in an ice-filled shaker tin. Shake vigorously. Strain into a chilled coupe glass.

Pairing: Coconut-Banana Macaroons, page 50

Sherry Flip

The flip is a cocktail made with a spirit or fortified wine that is shaken with sugar, a whole egg, and ice. It is frothy, rich, and delicious with or without the cream.

2 ounces sherry, such as oloroso
1 whole egg

1 teaspoon confectioners' sugar
1 ounce heavy cream (optional)
Freshly grated nutmeg

Combine the sherry, egg, confectioners' sugar, and cream, if desired, in shaker tin without ice. Dry shake for 30 seconds. Add ice to the shaker. Shake vigorously for 30 seconds more. Strain into a sour glass or wineglass and garnish with a grating of nutmeg.

Pairing: Sugarplums, page 23

MILK IT!
(ALTERNATIVE MILK BASICS)

It's difficult to keep up with the array of nondairy milks popping up on store shelves. It seems there are new ones every day. Soy milk was all the rage when it hit the stage four decades ago, and it seems like just a handful of years ago almond milk in a carton was the newest trend. Now grocery store dairy cases offer nut milk from cashews, walnuts, peanuts, and hazelnuts, as well as plant-based milks made from oats, flax, peas, quinoa, spelt, and hemp. You even can find blends like almond-oat and almond-coconut. With all those options, why make your own? Because it's easy and you can control the ingredients. Here are a few alternative milk basics worth mastering.

Nut Milk (1 pint)

Use this method with most any variety of nut. I prefer to lightly toast the nuts on a sheet pan in a single layer at 350°F for 10 minutes to bring out the flavor. No need to cool them. Just put the warm nuts in a bowl, cover with water, and let soak. A high-speed blender really helps things along. Many use cloth nut-milk bags to drain and squeeze all the liquid from the nuts, but layered cheesecloth over a strainer works well.

6 ounces raw nuts of choice, toasted

2 cups filtered water, plus more for soaking

¼ teaspoon Himalayan pink salt

½ to 1 teaspoon agave syrup or honey (optional)

Place the toasted nuts in a large mixing bowl. Pour water over the nuts to cover. Set aside in a cool place to soak 8 to 12 hours or overnight. Drain. Combine the nuts, 2 cups water, salt, and agave or honey, if using, in a high-speed blender for 3 minutes until smooth. Let mixture sit in blender for 5 minutes to allow solids to settle. Carefully pour the liquid through a cheesecloth-lined strainer. Scrape any remaining solids into the strainer. Gather up the corners of the cheesecloth and twist to squeeze as much remaining moisture from the nuts as possible. Transfer the strained milk to a jar and refrigerate up to 5 days.

FLAVORFUL ADDITIONS

Add any of the below to the blender to create flavored nut milks.

Vanilla Nut Milk: 2 teaspoons vanilla extract (or seeds from 1 scraped vanilla bean)

Chocolate Nut Milk: ¼ cup unsweetened extra-dark cocoa powder

Horchata: 1 tablespoon ground cinnamon

NOTE: Save leftover wet nut pulp to whirl into smoothies or dips like hummus, or dry the pulp in a single layer on a baking sheet in the oven on the lowest setting. Use the dried pulp as crumbs for breading meat or fish, or pulverize it further to make almond flour.

RESOURCES

BOOKS

The American Bar:
The Artistry of Mixing Drinks
Charles Schumann (1995)

Jerry Thomas Bartenders Guide
Jerry Thomas (1862)

Meehan's Bartender Manual
Jim Meehan (2017)

The Home Bartender: 125 Cocktails
Made with Four Ingredients or Less
Shane Carley (2016)

The Complete Guide to Cocktails and Drinks
Stuart Walton (2003)

The Southern Foodways Alliance
Guide to Cocktails
Sara Camp Milam and Jerry Slater (2017)

The Drunken Botanist
Amy Stewart (2013)

Beach Cocktails: Favorite Surfside Sips
and Bar Snacks
The Editors of *Coastal Living* (2017)

WEBSITES

https://www.alcademics.com/

https://www.supercall.com/

https://mrbostondrinks.com/

https://talesofthecocktail.com/

https://www.diffordsguide.com/

https://punchdrink.com/

https://www.cocktailsafe.org/

ACKNOWLEDGMENTS

Many thanks to my people: John, Parker, Ella, and Addie Cobbs, and so many friends for tasting, sipping, and commenting on the recipes in this book every step of the way. Much gratitude to eagle-eyed culinary pro Lyda Jones Burnette for testing and helping me fine-tune the recipe assortment. Let me raise a brimming glass to designer Matt Ryan for creating such a gorgeous cover and interiors. To my collaborators at Blueline Creative Group—Becky Stayner, Mindi Shapiro, Torie Cox, Katy Wohlfarth, and Elizabeth Howell—your talents made this book beautiful.

A wealth of gratitude goes to the restaurant managers and PR folks who were instrumental in getting me the recipes and interviews that I needed for this book, including Alexa Pavlovski, Emily Iscoff-Daigian, Gabrielle Gaines, Gavin Hatcher, Cathal Foley, Michelle Banovic, Jennifer Parnell, John Dye, Judith Rontal, Kayt Mathers, Lindsey Brown, and Vincent Ventura.

METRIC CHART

The recipes that appear in this cookbook use the standard United States method for measuring liquid and dry or solid ingredients (teaspoons, tablespoons, and cups). The information on this page is provided to help cooks outside the U.S. successfully use these recipes. All equivalents are approximate.

Metric Equivalents for Different Types of Ingredients

A standard cup measure of a dry or solid ingredient will vary in weight depending on the type of ingredient. A standard cup of liquid is the same volume for any type of liquid. Use the following chart when converting standard cup measures to grams (weight) or milliliters (volume).

STANDARD CUP	FINE POWDER (ex. flour)	GRAIN (ex. rice)	GRANULAR (ex. sugar)	LIQUID SOLIDS (ex. butter)	LIQUID (ex. milk)
1	140 g	150 g	190 g	200 g	240 ml
¾	105 g	113 g	143 g	150 g	180 ml
⅔	93 g	100 g	125 g	133 g	160 ml
½	70 g	75 g	95 g	100 g	120 ml
⅓	47 g	50 g	63 g	67 g	80 ml
¼	35 g	38 g	48 g	50 g	60 ml
⅛	18 g	19 g	24 g	25 g	30 ml

Useful Equivalents for Liquid Ingredients by Volume

¼ tsp					=	1 ml		
½ tsp					=	2 ml		
1 tsp					=	5 ml		
3 tsp	= 1 Tbsp			= ½ fl oz	=	15 ml		
	2 Tbsp	=	⅛ cup	= 1 fl oz	=	30 ml		
	4 Tbsp	=	¼ cup	= 2 fl oz	=	60 ml		
	5⅓ Tbsp	=	⅓ cup	= 3 fl oz	=	80 ml		
	8 Tbsp	=	½ cup	= 4 fl oz	=	120 ml		
	10⅔ Tbsp	=	⅔ cup	= 5 fl oz	=	160 ml		
	12 Tbsp	=	¾ cup	= 6 fl oz	=	180 ml		
	16 Tbsp	=	1 cup	= 8 fl oz	=	240 ml		
	1 pt	=	2 cups	= 16 fl oz	=	480 ml		
	1 qt	=	4 cups	= 32 fl oz	=	960 ml		
				33 fl oz	=	1000 ml	=	1 l

Useful Equivalents for Dry Ingredients by Weight

(To convert ounces to grams, multiply the number of ounces by 30.)

1 oz	= ¹⁄₁₆ lb	= 30 g
4 oz	= ¼ lb	= 120 g
8 oz	= ½ lb	= 240 g
12 oz	= ¾ lb	= 360 g
16 oz	= 1 lb	= 480 g

Useful Equivalents for Length

(To convert inches to centimeters, multiply the number of inches by 2.5.)

1 in			= 2.5 cm	
6 in	= ½ ft		= 15 cm	
12 in	= 1 ft		= 30 cm	
36 in	= 3 ft	= 1 yd	= 90 cm	
40 in			= 100 cm	= 1 m

Useful Equivalents for Cooking/Oven Temperatures

	FAHRENHEIT	CELSIUS	GAS MARK
Freeze water	32° F	0° C	
Room temperature	68° F	20° C	
Boil water	212° F	100° C	
Bake	325° F	160° C	3
	350° F	180° C	4
	375° F	190° C	5
	400° F	200° C	6
	425° F	220° C	7
	450° F	230° C	8
Broil			Grill

INDEX

ABOUT THE AUTHOR

KATHERINE COBBS is a writer, editor, and culinary professional with twenty-five years of experience. She collaborated with country music star Martina McBride on two cookbooks–*Around the Table* and *Martina's Kitchen Mix*–and produced books for multiple James Beard award-winning chefs, including two cookbooks for Chef Frank Stitt (*Frank Stitt's Southern Table* and *Frank Stitt's Bottega Favorita*), one for Iron Chef Chris Hastings (*Hot and Hot Fish Club Cookbook*), and one for Chef Todd English (*Cooking in Everyday English*). She created seventy-five all-new recipes for the hugely successful Garden & Gun *The Southerner's Cookbook*. Most recently she served as executive editor for Oxmoor House, an imprint of Time Inc. Books, where she worked on *The Southern Living Party Cookbook* and with Pulitzer Prize–winner and *New York Times* bestselling author Rick Bragg on *My Southern Journey*; TODAY Show contributor Elizabeth Heiskell on the bestselling *What Can I Bring?* cookbook; Southern gentleman Matt Moore on *The South's Best Butts*; Texas author and sommelier Jessica Dupuy on *United Tastes of Texas* and *United Tastes of the South*; and soulful Atlanta Chef Todd Richards on his critically acclaimed SOUL cookbook that was recently included as one of Amazon and *Publishers Weekly*'s Best Books of 2018.